iea Environment Working Paper

Global Greens, Global Governance

Jeremy Rabkin and James Sheehan

The Institute of
Economic Affairs

IEA Environment Working Paper No. 4

2 Lord North Street
London SW1P 3LB

ISBN   0 255 36472-5

Telephone: 0171 799 3745
Facsimile: 0171 799 2137
E-mail: enviro@iea.org.uk
Internet: www.iea.org.uk

Price £8.00 inc. P&P

Registered Charity
#235351
Company Registration
#755502

A Publication of the IEA Environment Unit

Foreword: Growing the Green Bureaucracy

The environmental slogan 'think globally, act locally' has been turned on its head in the nineties. Irrespective of what environmentalists have been thinking, their only notable successes have been international agreements. Environmental power and influence is shifting inexorably up the political hierarchy. To most, this development is seen as a thoroughly good thing, but there are good reasons to be wary of the environmental empire builders. The authors of the following working papers, Jeremy Rabkin and James Sheehan, demonstrate with devastating effect the numerous unaccountable facets of global politics.

The Green Power Grab

Government signatories to the UN Climate Convention who met recently in Buenos Aires claim they have taken a step toward saving the planet by setting limits on carbon dioxide emissions. The fact that science does not yet, and may never, support their belief of greenhouse-gas induced harm does not deter the bureaucrats from their mission. But not only is the aim of the Convention probably groundless, its side-effects are turning out to be far worse than critics first feared. The emerging concern is that UN-inspired international laws, such as the climate treaty, are undermining national sovereignty by handing power to interest groups and international bureaucrats.

How has this loss of sovereignty occurred with so few complaints? One theory is political sleight of hand, where one ingrained anxiety (nuclear war) has been skilfully substituted for another (environmental disaster).

It is far-fetched to suggest that some kind of supranational conspiracy planned for the environmental agenda to step in when the Soviet Union imploded. Although, as the joke goes, 'throw a socialist out the window and an environmentalist will walk in through the door'. But the incentives of the 'crisis entrepreneurs', the eco-pressure groups, the old defence bureaucracy and the new green bureaucracy, ensured that the void left by the Cold War was filled in the public mind. The scaremongering apparently worked, because the international community sighed with collective relief when the UN climate secretariat was established in the early nineties to tackle global warming.

In his 1982 book, 'Progress and Privilege', William Tucker set out the blueprint for bureaucratic expansion of power. Bureaucrats succeed he claimed, 'by extending the rules of society to cover as many aspects of life as possible'. By controlling emissions of carbon dioxide the climate treaty comes as close as possible to controlling life itself. Carbon dioxide is, after all, essential for all life on the planet, despite being considered a pollutant by the world's regulators. National governments have handed the climate secretariat power to determine what must be done and are glad to be rid of the moral responsibility. But international bureaucrats' best interests rarely coincide with those of the man in the street, or even of his government.

Margaret Maxey, Professor of Bioethics at the University of Texas in Austin,

1

claims that the whole UN process of bureaucratisation could lead to dissolution of independence among sovereign nations. This may precipitate their eventual replacement by a supranational realignment of power. By then, of course, it will be too late to protest that this isn't what voters wanted.

Eternal Bureaucracy

Establishing a treaty is only the beginning of the loss of sovereignty. Upon ratification, treaties become legally binding on nation states, yet they are typically altered years later. Such changes are made at the discretion of the secretariat, which frequently appropriates greater powers to itself and successful pressure groups. For example, under the auspices of the Montreal Protocol, ozone-depleting asthma inhalers are likely soon to be banned in Europe – a madness that would never had been agreed by the initial signatories in 1987. But the bureaucrats who banned the major CFC sources are now going after every last emission source. They use the highly contentious claim that skin cancer will be increased as a result of marginal reductions in stratospheric ozone to ensure the ozone-CFC issue stays alive and they keep their jobs.

In 'Global Greens', James Sheehan details other dangers of the expansion of unaccountable supranational bureaucracies. Sheehan explains that environmentalists and some corporations, who have restricted access to politicians at home, have far greater freedom to lobby politicians and international bureaucrats at UN meetings. He claims environmentalists unduly influence many UN agreements such as the Basle Convention on hazardous waste, which seriously undermines trade in scrap metal, and even donations of used clothes destined for the world's poor.

Many green groups that used to oppose UN and World Bank programmes have now been drawn into the bureaucracy by UN money, claims Sheehan. The result of this UN largesse and green hypocrisy is that at the 1997 Kyoto climate meeting there were 3,500 representatives from (predominantly European) pressure groups and only 1,500 delegates from member governments. Not surprisingly, therefore, Sheehan cites examples of third world participants at the UN meetings being repeatedly ignored in favour of alarmist 'eco-imperialist' greens, whose presence at the meeting was larger and more vocal.

Ironically, some green lobbying has led to regulations that will harm the environment. For example, the Convention on Biological Diversity supplants US regulations on biotechnology products with unscientific and more burdensome international regulations. Henry Miller, Senior Research Fellow at the Hoover Institution, says that such limits will significantly hamper research capable of supplying 'more plentiful and nutritious foods and biological alternatives to chemical pesticides and fertilisers'. The effect – more land goes under the plough, potentially reducing the area of important ecosystems.

Furthermore, the UN World Heritage Sites Convention, supposed to help third world governments protect their natural sites, has wound up being used against

Europeans and Americans. For example, the WHS UN secretariat disallowed a mining project 20 miles from Yellowstone Park because of concern (which was groundless) that the Park would be harmed. Montanan businessmen have been in a legal battle for years to begin mining because of the unnecessary UN involvement.

The US and EU delegates who recently jetted back from Buenos Aires probably consider they have brokered a good climate deal. The interests lobbying them at the meeting also left well satisfied, but they will have further reduced national sovereignty in favour of an unaccountable bureaucratic elite of which they are happy to be a part.

As Jeremy Rabkin explains in 'Morgen Die Welt', Europe is becoming increasingly bureaucratised and no constituency on this side of the Atlantic is likely to oppose the UN power grab. In fact, according to Rabkin, European political systems are the model for the UN. Worse still Rabkin explains how health treaties (devised by the World Health Organisation), may soon be tabled to mirror their environmental counterparts.

There is little doubt that the process towards global governance has begun. Rabkin concludes his paper by sketching three scenarios of where it may lead.

The IEA Environment Unit is delighted to present these two working papers. Please note that unlike other IEA publications, Working Papers are not subject to peer review; if you have comments or criticisms, please email them to us at <enviro@iea.org.uk>. As with all the Unit's publications, the views expressed are those of the authors and not of the Institute (which has no corporate view), its Trustees, Advisers or Directors.

Roger Bate, Co-Director, IEA Environment Unit

May 1999

About the Authors

Professor Jeremy Rabkin has a PhD from Harvard and is tenured at the Department of Government at Cornell University where he teaches international law and the politics of regulation. His latest book, 'Why Sovereignty Matters' was published by the American Enterprise Institute, Washington DC in 1998.

James M. Sheehan directs international policy activities at the Competitive Enterprise Institute, a non-profit think tank in Washington DC, that promotes free market and private property-based solutions to public policy issues. At CEI, Sheehan specialises in policies concerning international environmental regulation, trade, finance and foreign aid. His latest book, 'Global Greens: Inside the international environmental establishment' was published by the Capital Research Center in Washington DC in 1998.

3

MORGEN DIE WELT
Snaring the World in the EU's Green Vision

Jeremy Rabkin

The UN's 1992 Earth Summit was supposed to inaugurate a new era in world affairs. Held just after the dissolution of the Iron Curtain and the collapse of the Soviet Union, the conference sought to highlight new fields for international cooperation. It was, in fact, attended by more heads of state than any conference in the history of the United Nations.

Officially titled the *Conference on Environment and Development*, it sought to bridge the environmental concerns of developed nations and the economic concerns of less developed countries. Even siting the conference in the southern hemisphere – in Brazil's Rio de Janeiro, one of the burgeoning megacities of the developing world – was a gesture to North-South harmony. The conference endorsed the Rio Declaration on Environment and Development, a statement of shared principles which offered matching affirmations, almost in alternating paragraphs, of its two great aims – protecting the global environment and promoting growth in poor countries. These goals were linked under the harmonising slogan of 'sustainable development'.

The conference also featured a prominent role for non-governmental organisations (NGOs), whose tens of thousands of representatives far outnumbered the official delegates. This gesture to 'global civil society' was touted by many observers as a harbinger of a better world, a world in which visionary activists could transcend the narrow aims of their home states and prod national governments to address common concerns on a global basis.

Yet just beneath the surface, there were simmering conflicts. The rhetoric of sustainable development did not, after all, succeed in papering over sharp differences in priorities and perspectives. European delegates succeeded in writing into the Rio Declaration the so-called 'precautionary principle' that 'lack of full scientific certainty shall not be used as a reason for postponing cost-effective measures to prevent environmental degradation'. This principle, which seems to say that environmental concerns should always take precedence over competing risks or concerns, had already been written into German law in the 1980s and endorsed by the EU in the early 1990s. It was, in effect, Europe's gift to environmental policy – or at least, to policy rhetoric. But of the two great treaties, launched at Rio and supposed to embody this principle, the United States refused to make any commitment to one of them – the Convention on Biological Diversity. The United States did agree to sign the other, the Framework Convention on Climate Change, but only after the treaty text had been stripped of any definite commitments for action.

Meanwhile, tensions between developing and developed countries were even greater. Governments of less developed countries repeatedly warned that environmental protection should not come at the expense of their own economic development and, taking a more defiant stand than the American delegation, refused to consider climate change commitments of their own, even if postponed to subsequent negotiations. According to one observer, 'the gulf between the biggest environmental NGOs [those from Europe or North America] and many Southern NGOs in particular seemed almost as huge as that between their respective governments ...'[1] There was, in fact, a constant undertone of mutterings against western 'eco-imperialism'.

In many ways, Rio did indeed help to launch a new era in world affairs. It is an era in which programmes of international environmental regulation seem to have increasing appeal to some western governments – most notably in Europe. It is also an era in which these same programmes have proved to have much potential for exacerbating strains between the most affluent nations and those developing nations that used to be called 'the Third World'.

As it happens, the international prospect mirrors, in some ways, a debate now underway about the proper pace or intensity of integration within the European Union. Enthusiasts of deeper integration insist that the process will end the possibility of serious conflicts among the member states of the EU. Others warn that an overly ambitious agenda for common policy will inevitably exacerbate tensions, fanning diplomatic conflict and popular resentments, creating more opportunities for nationalist demagogues. Whichever side proves to be right within Europe, developments since Rio suggest that the world needs a more serious debate about the international counterpart to the European trend – the process, that is, by which western countries (and most particularly the EU countries) have been extending their own environmental concerns to the world at large.

Part I of this paper will sketch the reasons why the European Union has become a particularly persistent champion of international environmental programmes. Part II will sketch the resulting pattern, highlighting the concerns of less developed nations about the emerging direction of such ventures. Part III will offer some speculations on where this trend may lead. It may lead into a future that is far more dangerous and conflict-ridden than the hopeful affirmations at Rio would suggest.

---

[1] Michael Grubb, Matthias Koch, et. al., *The Earth Summit Agreements: A Guide and Assessment* (London: Earthscan Publications, 1993), p. 44. Some observers also note a differing emphasis, evident at the Rio Summit and more generally, between 'mainstream NGOs,' mostly U.S.-based and concerned to nurture practical solutions, versus more 'political' or 'consciousness-raising' NGOs, drawing their support from European Greens. Matthias Finger and Thomas Princen, *Environmental NGOs in World Politics: Linking the Local and the Global* (New York: Routledge, 1994) ('Introduction')

Part I: The European Difference

Why has the EU been such a consistent, determined champion of all recent ventures in international environmental regulation? A simple answer is that the member states of the EU are among the most affluent countries in the world. Environmental concern tends to be strongly correlated with wealth, both within countries and between them. This makes obvious intuitive sense: the more one is freed from preoccupation with food and shelter and security, the easier it is to value aesthetic, recreational or more remote health concerns.

But affluence alone does not explain the emerging pattern. The United States is certainly blessed with levels of economic success at least comparable to those achieved in Western Europe. But the United States has been a good deal more skittish or ambivalent about the larger trend. The United States, for example, has consistently tried to restrain EU enthusiasm for ambitious ventures in 'climate control', involving targeted reductions in greenhouse gases. While the Clinton administration did express support for the commitments spelled out in the 1997 Kyoto Protocol, this treaty has not been ratified by the US Senate and indeed faces strong opposition there. Nor has the Senate ratified the 1992 Convention on Biodiversity nor the 1989 Basle Convention on the shipment of hazardous wastes.

There are strong supporters of all these measures in the United States, particularly among environmentalist advocacy groups. But there are also strong and effective opposition forces in American politics. To a lesser but still notable extent, environmental advocates in Australia have also encountered strong political resistance, reflected in the much more cautious stance of the Australian government at the Kyoto negotiations, at subsequent negotiations on a Biosafety Protocol and in other international forums.

If affluence alone does not explain the strength of green advocacy in Europe, what does? Differences in national culture seem to be part of the explanation. Germany, the largest country in the EU, has enacted the world's most ambitious recycling laws and is home to the most politically successful Green Party. Ambitious environmental measures and avowedly environmentalist parties have also demonstrated strong appeal in the Netherlands and in Scandinavian countries, sharing similar cultural traditions. Polling data confirms the point. By very sizeable majorities, people in these countries tell pollsters they support strong environmental measures, even at some direct cost to themselves. Polling in the United States and Canada finds much more resistance to costly environmental measures. So, in a carefully constructed survey of 43 countries in the early 1990s, Sweden, Denmark, Netherlands scored at the top of the list with 'high' support for environmental protection from over 60 per cent of respondents; the United States and Canada were below the median, with high support from only 40 and 42 per cent respectively.[2]

---

[2] Ronald Inglehart, 'Public Support for Environmental Protection: Objective Problems and Subjective Values in 43 Societies,' *PS: Political Science & Politics*, March 1995, p. 61

What makes these differences particularly interesting is that they are related, in turn, to other cultural differences. Ronald Inglehart, a co-founder of the Euro-Barometer surveys who subsequently helped organise the World Values surveys in the early 1990s, has pored over survey results from dozens of countries on a whole range of issues. He reports – as casual observation already suggests – that the 'environmentalist cause is only one of many post-modern issues' favoured by the same constituencies. High levels of environmental concern turn out to be strongly correlated with new views on the status of women and families, immigrants and ethnic minorities, national symbols, religion and many other social issues. And 'the environmental cause has emerged as the symbolic centre of this broad cultural emancipation movement'.[3] This larger trend in opinion is quite as evident in North America as in northern Europe but it also confronts broader currents of opposition or resistance in America, where religion and older patterns of family life remain stronger.

Yet for all their suggestiveness, these cultural variations cannot account for the European difference in the international arena. For if there are important differences across the developed world, there are also quite important differences within the EU, itself. Green parties may be strong in northern Europe but they have little presence in southern Europe. Whatever the deep cultural inclinations of the Nordic nations, they are not deeply ingrained in the cultural background of the Latin nations or the Greeks. Polling results show wide variations among EU countries on levels of environmental concern. Inglehart finds Italy, France and Belgium – along with less affluent Spain, Portugal and Ireland – rank near the bottom of his 43 nation survey: in these six Catholic countries, fewer than half the proportion of respondents register high levels of support for environmental protection, compared with respondents in the Netherlands and Scandinavia.[4] There are also interesting differences in the background of post-modern social attitudes to which environmentalism is linked, as a political cause. Britain, for example, stands out in the polling data in its degree of popular endorsement for 'national pride' as Ireland does on the importance of faith in God, while the US and Canada stand out in both respects. [5]

So the question needs to be rephrased: what makes it possible for the EU, with all its internal divisions, to take such a strong stand, while the United States is hobbled by conflicting currents of opinion? The short answer is that the EU has

---

[3] Ronald Inglehart, *Modernization and Postmodernization, Cultural, Economic and Political Change in 43 Societies* (Princeton, N.J.: Princeton University Press, 1997), p. 244 (suggesting the relative salience of specifically environmental concerns in this 'cultural liberation' outlook reflects the political reality that 'while many of the other Postmodern causes tend to be divisive, practically everyone likes clean air and green trees. Although these [political movements] reflect an entire worldview, environmental symbols capture the issue on which they have the widest potential appeal').

[4] Inglehart, 'Public Support for Environmental Protection,' p. 61

[5] Inglehart, *Modernization and Postmodernization*, p. 86 (Results from the 'World Values' survey in the early 1990s: 55% of Britons tell pollsters they are 'very proud' of their nationality, compared with barely 20% in Germany and Netherlands, fewer than 40% in Italy, France, Belgium and Denmark – and 60% in Canada, 75% in the USA and 78% in Ireland. On the question whether God is 'very important' in their lives, 75% of Irish respondents say yes, compared with about 40% in Germany and Britain, 25% in France and fewer than 20% in Belgium, Sweden and Denmark – and 62% in Canada, 78% in the USA).

been quite effective as a broker of conflicting or competing impulses among member states. At most international conferences, the EU comes to the table with a common position, already settled among the member states in prior negotiations within the EU. At Kyoto, for example, Europeans pressed for an ambitious programme of emission reductions based on a prior agreement to share the burden within Europe. Under this scheme, EU countries prepared to make sharp cutbacks in greenhouse gas emissions would take some of the reduction burden from other EU countries which could not (or would not) commit to such emission cutbacks.

But this answer simply pushes off the ultimate question: why are European states able to cooperate in this way to reach a common EU position?

This requires a longer answer. It might be summed up in the claim that EU nations find it much easier to cooperate on international environmental measures, because these measures already mirror the way the EU operates, internally. Or, to put the point a bit differently, European nations are more inclined to support international programmes of environmental regulation because these programmes are, in many ways, an extension of the way the EU already does business at home. This is so in regard to the institutional arrangements for these programmes and still more in regard to their substantive policies and associated political characteristics.

To start with the most obvious and important institutional factor: Ambitious international programmes stir concerns in the United States and in many other countries about threats to national sovereignty. But not in Europe. Most politicians in Europe have become quite comfortable with the idea of 'pooled sovereignty'. To the extent that international regulatory schemes commit national governments to ongoing ventures, most of these ventures are, after all, rather modest compared to the grand venture of European integration, itself.

The institutional characteristics of new environmental schemes are also quite familiar to Europeans. The most ambitious ventures tend to start with a general framework convention, which is then given successively more precision in subsequent agreements or protocols. It is more than a process of fitting details to general standards. It is rather a technique of articulating a political consensus and then using this initial commitment to constrain subsequent bargaining. And this is just how the EU handles its own environmental planning. The European Commission formulates five year 'action plans'. These are then implemented in subsequent Commission directives that gain momentum and credibility from the non-binding 'plans'.

Even where international programmes rely on international administrative authorities – rather than subsequent rounds of treaty negotiation – this is nothing new for EU countries. The most striking feature of the EU polity is the extent to which major policy initiatives are delegated to the European Commission, in a system where the European Parliament has few formal powers to direct or discipline the bureaucrats.

But the institutional affinities are probably much less important than the policy parallels. Within the EU, environmental policy is extremely attentive to distributional effects on business. Business is a major constituency of EU level 'harmonisation' policies – in the environmental field, as elsewhere. Business lobbying is certainly a standard feature of politics in all democratic countries. But it is central to the way the EU operates, because the project of European integration is so much more ambitious.

Free trade across state borders was guaranteed in the US Constitution in 1787. In Europe, the reduction of trade barriers has been a highly contentious project of recent decades. High-wage countries have worried about the effect of opening their markets to countries with lower average wages. So, too, countries with higher environmental or regulatory standards have worried about the effect of opening their markets to firms operating in countries with less demanding standards. The environmental standards of the EU are, in part, a way of protecting the competitive interests of countries with more ambitious environmental norms. As one recent study observed, 'the European Union has become a vehicle for exporting the environmental standards of Europe's greener nations to the rest of the continent'.[6]

Thus, EU interest in environmental regulation really gained prominence only with the advent of the Single European Act of 1987, which set out to eliminate all barriers to cross-border trade with in Europe – and, to achieve this goal, promised a systematic harmonisation of standards on a wide range of domestic regulations. The number of environmental directives in the period 1989-91 exceeded all those issued in the preceding 20 years. DG XI, the directorate of the European Commission with special responsibility for environmental regulation, expanded from 55 staff in 1986 to 450 in 1992.[7] Summarising a number of more detailed studies, a recent survey of EU policy making concludes that 'of the main influences, economic motives seem to provide the most important authority behind the development of European environmental policy'.[8] Among other things, it is notable that the Commission prefers to invoke treaty provisions which mandate uniform standards, rather than those which would require states to reach a minimum standard of environmental protection and then leave it to local authorities to do more, if they wish.

The point is not that European environmental regulation is simply a sham to cover business protectionism. But it is clear, at least, that the EU is extremely alert to the commercial implications of particular environmental standards. In the North American Free Trade Agreement, by contrast, there is no provision for harmonising environmental standards and no institutional machinery to secure common standards. Instead, each of the three NAFTA countries is bound simply by vague commitments not to lower environmental standards or deliberately under-enforce its own existing laws for the sake of trade advantages against the others. The EU, on the other hand, has worked, systematically and deliberately, to extend

---

[6] David Vogel, *Trading Up: Consumer and Environmental Regulation in a Global Economy* (Harvard University Press, 1996), p. 97
[7] Justin Greenwood, *Representing Interests in the European Union* (London: Macmillan, 1997), p. 181
[8] Id at 183

the standards favoured by some EU states to all the others. It is very natural, therefore, for the EU to look to international environmental standards as a way of extending its favoured policies still more broadly.

Apart from overriding attention to the commercial implications of environmental regulation, the EU has also pioneered, in its own internal affairs, two other features of regulatory politics that play a prominent part in global environmental negotiations. One is the special provision made for non-governmental advocacy groups. The EU has been a remarkably eager patron of NGOs, in the environmental field, as elsewhere and it has special incentives to cultivate these groups.

The basic structure of the EU generates continual tensions between European institutions and the governments of the EU's member states. Both the European Parliament and the European Commission therefore seek to promote advocacy groups with a European outlook, groups which can then act as champions of EU policy within the member states. Nearly ten per cent of the EU budget now goes to the funding of such groups. Environmental advocacy groups have been notable beneficiaries of the larger pattern.[9]

Thus about one in five European-wide interest advocacy groups represents non-profit 'public interest' concerns and a 1996 survey found that these groups tend to have more permanent staff and higher budgets than the more numerous business lobbying groups.[10] The European Environmental Bureau, representing a network of national advocacy groups in Brussels, receives about half its funding from direct EU grants. Of the six other large environmental advocacy groups with headquarters in Brussels, all but Greenpeace acknowledge receiving sizeable portions of their operating budgets from the European Commission.[11] While Greenpeace is quite reticent about revealing its funding sources, it does acknowledge that the bulk of its revenue comes from Germany and Scandinavia, while it actually spends more in the United States than it collects there.[12]

The European Parliament, in which Greens achieved the status of the fourth largest party in 1989, has been eager to tap into public support for environmental

---

[9] In 1996, the EU channelled 9.25 per cent of its total budget to the non-profit, non-governmental sector, according to A.M. Agraa, *The European Union - History, Institutions, Economics and Policies* (London, Prentice Hall Europe, 1998), p. 319 Most of the money goes to private groups offering services to the poor, the unemployed, the disabled, ethnic minorities, etc. But environmental advocacy groups also take some share of this bounty. For example, the EU's 'Fourth Framework Research Programme' (1994-1998) budgeted 11.6 billion ECU for this period, almost all of it for work by outside organizations or institutions: about 15 per cent of this funding went to organizations studying either 'environment' issues (8.3 per cent) or 'cooperation' with non-EU countries and with international organizations (6.8 per cent). B. Harvey, *Networking in Europe: A Guide to European Voluntary Organisations*, 2d ed. (London: NCVO Publications and Community Development Foundation, 1995) provides these and further breakdowns (Ch. 3).

[10] Greenwood, p. 179

[11] Id, p. 186. DG XI (the EU Commission Directorate responsible for environmental policy) distributed grants totalling 7 million ECU to non-governmental organizations; in 1995, EEB's share of this largesse reached 409,477 ECU, by which time it had 'institutionalised its presence across a range of [EU] advisory committee structures'.

[12] According to its 1996 *Annual Report*, Greenpeace International received more than half of the revenue required for its international operation, headquartered in Amsterdam, from sources (not further itemized) in Germany. It operates at a deficit in the U.S., as well as in France and Japan and less developed countries (including China). Surpluses to fund these deficits come from UK, Canadian and Swedish sources, as well as (most massively) from Germany.

concerns by acting as a patron for environmental advocacy groups. The European Commission, anxious to diversify its sources of information and support, has routinely sought reports from non-governmental sources. Environmental advocacy groups now have an institutionalised role as suppliers of policy data and advice to the Commission. And they have learned how to operate strategically in Brussels. Even Greenpeace, better known elsewhere for staging sensational protest events, has learned to play by Brussels rules in the EU capital: it has, for example, commissioned research studies from local consulting firms, known to be suppliers of policy research to the European Commission.

The same advocacy groups have also taken an extremely prominent role in international negotiations, where environmental conferences give them special rights of participation. The 1992 Rio Summit was, by design, as much a forum for highlighting the concerns of non-governmental organisations (NGOs) as for facilitating the efforts of official state representatives. A recent UN study notes that the pattern only gained momentum thereafter: 'In the interlinked global conferences that have followed the Rio meeting, NGOs continued to have a strong impact on both the preparatory processes and the conferences. ... More and more, NGOs are helping to set the public policy agenda – identifying and defining critical issues and providing policymakers with advice and assistance'.[13] What these groups also do, of course, is to help mobilise public opinion, at least in the western countries where they have their greatest support.

A final feature of EU policy is the scheme of regional adjustments. Such redistribution efforts have long been a feature of domestic politics in Germany and other countries. Still, it is notable that they were so readily adapted to planning and policy at the European level. With two centuries of history as a single nation, the United States does not even now have any programme avowedly aimed at equalising wealth among the states of the American union. But the EU has tried to push ambitious integration programmes very far, very fast. In fact, EU harmonisation policies are, in many ways, more ambitious than federal regulatory policy in the United States. In the US, as in other federal countries, representatives of states with differing policies often succeed in blocking proposed federal policies that would override local policy preferences. In Europe, payments from the EU's cohesion fund for depressed regions have been a way of building support for common policies. In particular, such massive transfer payments have eased opposition to ambitious environmental norms from the less affluent EU states, notably Spain, Portugal, Ireland and Greece (which qualify for sizeable grants from a special cohesion fund). By the mid-1990s, almost a third of the EU budget was devoted to 'structural expenditures' on regional equalisation, with total outlays for the period 1994-99 projected to reach 178 billion ECUs.[14]

---

[13] Report of the Commission on Global Governance, *Our Global Neighbourhood* (Oxford University Press, 1995), p. 255. So, for example, the European Environment Bureau (EEB), an umbrella organization for dozens of smaller advocacy groups, was part of the official EU Commission delegation at the 1992 Rio Summit and at subsequent conferences on climate change and biodiversity. (Greenwood, p. 186)

[14] Greenwood, p. 221

Just this sort of policy has been introduced into a number of international environmental agreements – though on a much smaller scale – to buy support from less developed countries. Beginning in the mid-1960s, LDCs have repeatedly sought to use UN forums to build support for large scale wealth transfers from the rich nations of the 'North' to the poor countries of the 'South'. For more than two decades, these efforts were continually rebuffed by western countries (most vocally by the United States but in the end, just as decidedly by Western European countries). Recent environmental conferences, however, have sought to tap into continuing eagerness among poor countries for sustained programmes of international assistance. The Rio Conference was officially the *UN Conference on Environment and Development* – with the last part of the name designed to attract interest from developing countries. Individual treaties often do have some special incentive or sweetener for LDC participation, including special assistance funds and provisions for technology transfers. The scale is much smaller than in the EU but the policy impulse is similar: if less affluent countries resist the preferred policies of the rich countries, the rich can offer financial inducements to get dissidents to go along.

To sum up, then: international environmental regulation mirrors EU internal policies in some crucial institutional features – most notably, in the drive for common internal policies, prodded by ongoing conferences that sometimes feature majority voting (rather than consensus) and delegation of authority to centralised administrative units. In policy and politics, the affinities are still closer, as international policies become entangled in the pursuit of commercial advantage for some countries over others, while trying to mobilise broader support by subsidising non-profit advocacy groups and offering side-payments to dissident states. What Germany and a few other northern countries have done in the EU, the EU is now doing to the rest of the world: pressing to make its own policies the wider norm, so its own policy is less vulnerable to competition or local challenge.

We are still at an early stage in 'globalising' the preferred environmental policies of the EU, but it is already clear that this process is raising qualms in other western countries – and much suspicion and resistance from less developed countries.

Part II: Environmental Initiatives of the Past Decade

a) The Setting: WTO and the trade nexus

Before looking at particular environmental programmes, it is necessary to take note of their setting. International negotiations on environmental issues try to emphasise common concerns, but divisions between different regions have not disappeared. They have instead been channelled into new international fora.

Environmental issues did not emerge as a major topic of international negotiation until the end of the 1980s. But tensions between the affluent West and the impoverished South have a much longer history. Almost all the former colonies of Europe emerged as independent states in the first two decades after World War II. By the mid-1960s, non-western countries had attained a decisive majority in the United Nations. They accordingly sought to use the United Nations as a forum to pursue their demands for greater economic assistance from the affluent nations of the developed West. In 1964, the UN established a permanent UN Conference on Trade and Development (UNCTAD). A broad coalition of developing countries organised themselves into the Group of 77 (G-77) to urge fundamental changes in the terms of international trade. A decade later, the ambitions of UNCTAD and the G-77 coalesced into an elaborate programme, dubbed the New International Economic Order. Proponents envisioned a network of new international agreements which would assist developing countries with price supports for their basic commodity exports and also provide for systematic transfers of technology and resources from affluent nations to the developing world.

Western countries rejected this vision, however. Instead, they pursued new agreements to remove existing barriers to international trade, under the framework established by the General Agreement on Tariffs and Trade (GATT) in 1947. By the end of the 1980s, even most developing countries had come around to the view that trade liberalisation would serve their own interests, as the dramatic growth of free-trading states like Chile and Singapore showed what could be accomplished. While UNCTAD floundered on the sidelines, most countries in the world participated in negotiations in the early 1990s, aimed at replacing the GATT framework with a more formalised organisation, the World Trade Organisation. By the time it came into effect in 1995, the WTO had 128 members (compared with two dozen signatories of the original GATT rules of 1947).

By then, however, some western countries were having second thoughts about the basic trading rules of the GATT system. In 1992, the European Parliament, for example, called on the EU to establish protective duties against 'environmental dumping'[15] – the sale of goods at lower prices, when they have been produced in countries with inadequate environmental safeguards (and therefore, presumably, lower production costs). Developing countries strongly protested this idea, insisting

---

[15] Resolution A3-0329/92. A more modest proposal, authorizing special tariffs on goods produced in countries that did not conform to US air quality standards, was soundly defeated in the US Senate in 1990 (Sen. Amend. 1321).

it was no more than an excuse to protect European producers from outside competition. And 'eco-dumping' duties were certainly improper under the existing GATT rules, which allowed countries to exclude imports based on health or safety concerns about the products, themselves, but not on the basis of objections to the way the goods were produced in their home countries. The agreement establishing the WTO ended up with rhetorical gestures to the goal of sustainable development but no change in this traditional rule.

Some western governments remained dissatisfied. At the signing ceremonies for the WTO agreement in the spring of 1994, French President Chirac called on the new organisation to find some way to allow countries with high environmental and labour standards to protect themselves against 'unfair competition' from countries with deficient standards in these areas. The proposal was echoed by US Vice-President Gore, at a time when American labour and environmental groups were expressing sharp doubts about the WTO.

Meanwhile, many governments called attention to the awkward fact that a number of recent environmental agreements were already in conflict with WTO rules, since these agreements contemplated trade restrictions or trade sanctions which were not permissible (or so it seemed) under WTO rules. A new WTO Committee on Trade and Environment was established under the WTO and set out, as its first task, to resolve this immediate challenge.

Five years later, it has still not happened. Part of the reason is that the EU and the US could not agree on a common approach to the problem. In the United States, many environmental advocacy groups demanded an approach that would leave the US free to impose trade sanctions on its own authority – as it had done (and then found itself condemned by a GATT arbitration panel) in excluding tuna caught by ocean drift nets shown to be inadvertently snaring prized dolphins. The EU had engaged in such unilateral ventures of its own, most notably in trying to exclude the importation of fur when obtained from animals caught by leg traps (principally in Canada and Russia). But EU trade negotiators were more concerned to restrain American unilateralism than to protect EU prerogatives in this respect. So the EU pressed for a direct linkage between multi-lateral environmental agreements and trade standards. Sir Leon Brittan, Trade Commissioner for the EU, issued a series of warnings against 'green protectionism' if the WTO did not work out reasonable rules for a multilateral approach.[16] The Clinton administration vacillated, torn between its concern to protect the trading system and its eagerness to conciliate domestic environmentalists.

More important than American hesitation, however, was the unexpectedly strong opposition from less developed countries. They had signed a series of environmental agreements which, on their face, were in some tension with rules of

---

[16] See, e.g., the report of Commissioner Brittan's remarks before a committee of the European Parliament in 'WTO rules must not thwart environmental agreements,' *Europe Environment*, No. 524, June 9, 1998. The report also notes that some MEPs urged bans on 'cheap imports from countries enforcing lower animal welfare standards than the EU,' but 'Sir Leon suggested there are limits to what other countries can be coerced into doing'.

the trading system. Now they insisted that the trade rules should not be reformulated to accommodate full enforcement or implementation of these same agreements. Part of the reason was that LDCs feared that environmental standards would be coupled or soon followed with labour standards and a series of other measures designed to protect the markets of Europe and North America from their exports. So they insisted that trade rules should be kept quite separate from non-trade issues, but they has also developed a good deal more scepticism about the way environmental agreements had come to work, in practice, when urged along by the agitational skills of western environmental advocacy groups and the strategic calculation of western governments.

It is telling that as LDCs opposed mixing non-trade issues with trading rules, they also opposed the demands of environmental NGOs for greater openness in the WTO and a more assured place for NGO participation. NGOs had sought and won a prominent role in environmental treaty negotiations. Most G-77 countries were determined to deny NGOs any similar status at the WTO. So far, NGOs have indeed been kept at a distance and WTO rules have not been changed. Trade disputes continue to be settled by arbitration panels whose proceedings – and parallel efforts at voluntary settlement – are conducted in secret (though panel rulings are made public).

The WTO recently organised a forum at which NGOs could discuss their concerns about the operation of the trading system and its relation to environmental concerns. Most western states (and the EU) sent their trade ministers or top officials; almost no country from the old G-77 did so.17 The experience of LDCs with international environmental agreements and international environmental advocacy groups goes far in explaining such chilly attitudes.

b) Direct Trade Restraints – CITES and the Basle Convention

The 1973 Convention on International Trade in Endangered Species (CITES) is the oldest of the modern ventures in international environmental regulation. At the outset, it seemed to be relatively non-controversial. The treaty established a mechanism to assist conservation efforts for endangered species. Where some signatories sought help in suppressing the seizure of endangered species within their own borders, all other signatories could agree to suppress importation of such species – and so, it was hoped, suppress the demand that drove illegal poaching or harvesting.

The most ambitious application of the system developed in the 1980s, when western environmentalists began to emphasise the threat to African elephants. The Worldwide Fund for Nature was so intent on protecting elephants, that it financed the purchase of attack helicopters by local game wardens in Zimbabwe, resulting in

---

[17] 'WTO: First Ever Environmental Symposium Gets Underway,' *Greenwire* (electronic service of the *National Journal* of Washington, D.C.), March 16, 1999, citing the observation of a journalist from India: 'The scepticism of the developing countries shows in that only their Geneva-based ambassadors are attending the symposium,' while other countries sent high level officials.

the deaths of over fifty people thought to be engaged in poaching. Other western organisations helped African governments to hire British and South African mercenaries to train and lead anti-poacher hit squads, resulting in the deaths of several dozen poachers in Kenya from a new 'shoot on sight' policy.[18] News of these practices provoked a chorus of denunciations, however – at least in Africa. Western advocacy groups accordingly switched their attention to a new technique of control. The culminating effort, achieved in 1989, was a ban on the importation of ivory, which was supposed to rob poachers of their economic incentive to kill elephants.

The scheme inspired great enthusiasm – and was a fund-raising success for western environmentalists. But it never worked properly. On the one hand, smuggled ivory (for jewellery) and rhino horn (for Asian medicinal formulas) continued to find markets in Asian countries. On the other hand, the ban hobbled efforts to give local people a stake in protecting elephants – which can be very destructive to agriculture – when they were hobbled in finding ways to assure commercial value to the elephants. Countries in southern Africa repeatedly requested the CITES signatories to lift the ban during the course of the 1990s. They were able to show that programmes providing market-based incentives had enlisted much local cooperation and produced a considerable increase in elephant herds in their territories, while conventional conservation efforts in Kenya had not halted a continuing decline in elephant populations.

It took the better part of a decade, however, before the requisite two-thirds majority of CITES signatories would go along with even a modest lifting of the ban. Very few countries have elephants or face any direct burden from the ban, but donors in western countries, where environmental advocacy groups do the bulk of their fund-raising, are easily moved by impassioned appeals to save the elephants. Some environmental advocacy groups and animal-rights groups resisted to the end.[19] So countries that wanted to pursue a better programme for saving their own wildlife turned out to be hostage to an international regime they had not understood, when they signed up for it in the 1970s.

Meanwhile, western advocacy groups were also instrumental in getting international support for a different system of constraints on trade – the 1989 Basle Convention on transboundary shipment of hazardous waste. In practice, CITES has served to limit exports from less-developed countries. Basle, in a kind of mirror image, was explicitly designed to limit shipments from developed countries in the other direction. Greenpeace was particularly active in highlighting the danger that

---

[18] Raymond Bonner, *At the Hand of Man* (New York: Knopf, 1993), pp. 126-27, 155-57

[19] Wendy Marston, 'The Misguided Ivory Ban and the Reality of Living with Elephants,' *Washington Post,* June 8, 1997, p. C2, reporting the continuing opposition of World Wildlife Fund to a lifting of the ban, even while WWF acknowledged that elephants should no longer be listed as 'endangered'. People for the Ethical Treatment of Animals also opposed lifting the ivory ban, for fear it would encourage hunting (which was, indeed, the intention of villagers in Zimbabwe and elsewhere, seeking revenue from selling hunting licenses to sportsmen). A wildlife consultant in South Africa protested that European advocacy groups respond to 'the generosity of donors who feel sentimental about elephants or rhinos, but often show no compassion for people living in Africa'. Anton Ferreira, 'Africans See anti-ivory ban as foreign meddling,' Reuters World Service, Nov. 6, 1994

western countries would use poor countries as dumping grounds for hazardous waste. African countries indeed organised their own regional accord in 1991 (the Bamaco Agreement), imposing stricter limits on the importation of hazardous materials.

But the Basle Convention was not simply a matter of altruism on the part of western countries. If the concern was that receiving countries would not have adequate facilities for the safe handling of hazardous materials, the obvious solution was a system of export licenses, dependent on certification of such facilities at designated destinations. Instead, the parties to the Basle Convention soon organised a strict, two-tiered system, with a short list of western countries in one list and all other signatories in the other. Western countries then imposed strict prohibitions on the shipment of designated materials to other countries. How strictly this system could be enforced was shown in 1998, when the A-list countries rejected applications from Israel and Monaco to receive shipments of the listed materials. In effect, the Convention has operated as a reprocessing cartel for a small group of western countries.[20]

And there is much at stake. The waste removal industry earns $50 billion per year. Germany and a few other EU countries have invested heavily in recycling. Thus, some provincial governments within Germany have actually tried to restrict shipment of recyclables from one part of Germany to another, simply to ensure that business stays at local sites.[21]

Initial proposals would have included even scrap metal on the list of exports required to stay in top-tier countries. It has not yet gone that far, but the mechanisms are in place and they operate by majority vote – of the A-list countries. Characteristically, the United States has so far remained aloof from the Basle Convention (because of opposition in the US Senate). So European countries, long the most insistent promoters of this international control scheme, retain most influence on its direction.

Since the GATT is supposed to place sharp limits on export controls as well as import barriers, there is much question about whether Basle is consistent with WTO rules. Similar questions can be raised about ivory bans if they distinguish between ivory exports on the basis of their domestic conservation techniques. No complaint has yet been brought to the WTO to test the legality of these treaties. But given their experience, it is not surprising that LDCs have resisted a clarification of WTO rules that would give explicit authorisation to enforcement of these treaties. LDCs are not at all eager to give up the possibility, as a last resort, of lodging WTO complaints against western discrimination under these treaties.

---

[20] 'Parties to Basle Convention Adopt Two-List System for Waste Export,' BNA *International Environment*, March 4, 1998, p. 185, noting that the decision was strongly supported by Greenpeace International, which took the same position as the European governments.
[21] Vogel, *Trading Up*, p.

c) Protecting the atmosphere: Ozone and Climate Change

CITES and Basle raise special problems because they are explicitly about trade restraints. On the other hand, it can be argued that international agreements are most appropriate when it comes to shipment of products across international boundaries. Neither CITES nor Basle tries to regulate what countries do within their own borders. The most ambitious environmental ventures have precisely this characteristic – they try to regulate what goes on within each country, on the premise that what goes into the atmosphere cannot be confined within national borders.

The 1987 Montreal Protocol (expanding the Vienna Convention of 1985) on Ozone Depleting Chemicals has become the new model. It was a response to scientific studies, beginning in the 1970s, which found that the ozone layer in the upper atmosphere was thinning over Antarctica, as ozone molecules were broken down, probably by reactions with manmade chemicals. Chlorofluorocarbons (CFCs), commonly used in aerosol sprays and refrigerants, were thought to be particular culprits. Environmental advocacy groups seized on initial scientific speculations and trumpeted the warning that the erosion of the ozone layer in the atmosphere would allow much more ultra-violet light to reach the earth's surface, leading to increases in skin cancer around the world.

Such warnings were enough to prompt Western governments to organise a coordinated response. So a framework treaty, the Vienna Convention on Substances that Deplete the Ozone Layer, was negotiated in 1985. This initial treaty proposed only a general commitment to reduce reliance on the offending chemicals, without specific reduction targets or deadlines. Even so, it had only twenty signatories – all from developed countries. More scare stories (which soon proved exaggerated) were given much publicity by environmental advocacy groups.[22] Then a number of chemical companies, in Europe and the United States, began to support stronger curbs, when they realised a faster phase-out of CFCs would create a new market for substitutes – produced by western companies.

Even so, Britain supported the US government's call for a phase-out of 'inessential uses' of CFCs (as in aerosol sprays). Germany, with its large chemical industry and mobilised Green activists, demanded more comprehensive action. The Germans soon managed to rally most other EU states to their view,[23] however, less developed countries, led by India and China, remained sceptical.

The Montreal Protocol of 1987 responded to European demands for a definite international commitment to ending the use of ozone depleting substances, while

---

[22] Careful studies did not find that ozone depletion corresponded to ground-level increases in Ultraviolet B radiation, as alarmist forecasts had predicted. Joseph Scotto et. al., 'Biologically Effective Ultraviolet Radiation: Surface Measurements in the United States, 1974 to 1985,' *Science*, February 12, 1988 and the evidence linking seasonal ozone thinning to human activities was called into question by subsequent studies. S.F. Singer, 'Ozone Depletion Theory,' *Science*, Aug. 17, 1993

[23] Richard Elliot Benedick, *Ozone Diplomacy, New Directions in Safeguarding the Planet* (Cambridge, Mass: Harvard University Press, 1991), p. 39. The German Environment Minister at the time, Klaus Topfer, was subsequently rewarded for his success in pushing through a more ambitious control scheme: in the early 1990s, he became head of the United Nations Environment Programme.

the less developed countries refused for a time to endorse this commitment. The breakthrough came in the 1990 London Amendments, under which (in addition to tightening and speeding up commitments to stop the use of ozone depleting substances), western countries offered to create a fund to assist less developed countries in making the transition to new refrigerants. It was the first time that compliance with an environmental norm had been linked explicitly with compensating transfer payments – applying, in effect, the EU's internal approach to the world at large. Subsequent amendments to the Montreal Protocol, adopted in Copenhagen in 1992, also confirmed another sweetener for LDCs: tightened deadlines for the elimination of CFC use and production in developed countries would not apply to LDCs until 2010. For China, India and Mexico, the main remaining producers of CFCs, this offered the prospects of considerable gains, as the shutdown of production elsewhere worked a tripling of the price (and opened a black-market for smuggling even into western countries where CFC use was supposed to be ended by 1996).

The less developed countries have continued to protest – down to the latest conference of the parties at the end of 1998 – that transition funds made available do not remotely cover the costs of shifting to new refrigerants.[24] Refrigerants are not a matter of marginal comfort in poor countries. Without proper refrigeration, it is difficult to preserve food. Concerns were also expressed about protecting antibiotics and other medicines requiring refrigeration. In countries with poor transportation systems and limited government resources, even small changes in refrigeration capacity could have very alarming consequences.

Despite all this, most countries have felt obliged to ratify the Montreal Protocol, because signatories are pledged to observe trade restrictions (on servicing equipment using CFCs and on receiving imported goods made with CFCs) in their dealings with non-signatories. So even the truculent government of Myanmar (Burma) finally signed the Montreal Protocol in 1994, acknowledging that 'one of the major motivating factors' was 'the desire to avoid trade restrictions'.[25]

Meanwhile, the benefits of the undertaking are far from clear, especially for poor countries. The thinning of the ozone layer occurred in the polar regions, so it was feared was that effects would be felt by people in the higher latitudes of the northern and southern hemispheres. People living at lower latitudes (where almost

---

[24] 'Report of the Tenth Meeting of the Parties to the Montreal Protocol,' Cairo, 23-24 November 1998 (UNEP/OzL.Pro.10/9) Par. 43: 'Many representatives stated that existing levels of financial assistance to developing countries were insufficient to achieve the goals of the Protocol and said it was essential to ensure adequate and timely funding ...'. Meanwhile, UNEP Director Klaus Topfer 'urged donor countries to pay the balance of their contributions to the Multilateral Fund for 1998 and earlier years' (without reporting the extent of the shortfall). (Par. 9) A study by the World Bank estimated the cost of eliminating ozone depleting substances in China alone would reach US$14 billion by 2010. Ian Rowlands, *The politics of global atmosphere change* (Manchester: Manchester University Press, 1995), p. 184. By the end of 1998, the Multilateral Fund had authorized payments of some $220 million – for all countries eligible – while the World Bank had authorized an additional $300-$400 million. (Tenth Meeting Minutes, Par. 33, 36) China itself has received only $30 million.

[25] Rowlands, *politics of global atmosphere*, p. 183. The Austrian delegate to the ozone negotiations summed up the ultimatum presented to LDCs: 'Unless you join, you won't get those substances you need to meet your domestic needs ... [and because technology transfers are prohibited to non-Parties] countries not signing the Protocol will be unable to produce their own'. (Rowlands, p. 170)

19

all LDCs are situated) have always been exposed to higher levels of UV radiation. Ground-level exposure to ultra-violet radiation increases by about one per cent per mile as one moves from the poles to the Equator. Even the worst case scenario projected by UN scientific advisory panels – a ten per cent increase in ultra-violet exposure, due to ozone depletion – would be equivalent to moving 60 miles closer to the Equator.[26] So to ensure that populations in the affluent temperate zones did not face marginal increases in ultra-violet exposure, countries in poor, tropical regions, already facing more than that level of exposure, were asked to make disproportionate sacrifices. Even the off-setting gains to the few CFC producers among LDCs are scheduled to end by 2010.

Yet for all its dubious accomplishments, this scheme was touted, from the beginning, as a model for coping with the next great menace – the threat of global warming from the build-up of 'greenhouse gases'. The theory was that increasing concentrations of such gases in the atmosphere would trap heat at the earth's surface, leading to a gradual warming of the planet. After water vapour, the main greenhouse gas is carbon-dioxide, some of which is released by the burning of fossil fuels – that is, by the ordinary activities of life in industrial societies.[27] Environmentalists warned that as average temperatures rose, weather patterns might alter, leading to drought in some regions and catastrophic hurricanes in other regions. Some scientists even warned that a warming trend could lead to the melting of polar ice, raising sea levels and flooding coastal regions throughout the world.

To forestall such calamitous consequences, environmentalists urged a dramatic cut-back in the use of fossil fuels, in order to reduce the build-up of greenhouse gases. Of course, this policy would have severe economic consequences for most countries, but for a few European countries, the policy would not be so disturbing. By the early 1990s, a reunified Germany was busily dismantling inefficient and highly polluting coal-powered plants in the former East Germany. In Britain, the Thatcher government was consolidating its victory over the miners' union by privatising the coal industry and encouraging a nation-wide programme of transition from coal to more efficient oil and natural gas. Both the German and

---

[26] On the eve of the negotiations leading to the Montreal Protocol, an official UK government report noted that even if the worst of 'the postulated ozone depletion did occur, it would result in increased exposure [to UV-B radiation] equivalent to a person moving from northern to southern England'. The chief American negotiator, in his subsequently published account of these negotiations, reports this claim without disputing its truth. He instead responds that the UK argument 'missed the distinction between a voluntary move made with no knowledge of radiation consequences and the involuntary subjection of entire populations to known increases'. He does not speculate on how many Britons might be deterred from moving to southern England if the 'hazards' involved were better known. Benedick, *Ozone Diplomacy*, p. 38

[27] Ironically, the ozone layer is also thought to contribute to the trapping of heat at lower levels of the atmosphere. To the extent that earlier international agreements are successful in protecting the ozone layer, they may exacerbate the problem of global warming. This point is not denied but is rarely acknowledged by environmental advocates. Meanwhile, one of the main substitute chemicals for CFC – hydrochlorofluorocarbons (HCFCs) – are now thought to be a greenhouse gas, independently contributing to global warming. Environmentalists have demanded a rapid phasing out of HCFC use to avert global warming, while still refusing to countenance a return to reliance on CFCs. Similarly, if burning of fossil fuels is a major problem, the obvious alternative is to increase reliance on nuclear power, which does not produce greenhouse emissions. But environmental advocacy groups, long hostile to nuclear power, have not changed their position. If nothing else, the refusal of environmental advocates to establish clear priorities reflects a refusal to think in terms of trade-offs and hard choices and a preference for all-embracing ideological or theological commitments.

20

British governments thus took up the call for a world-wide reduction of greenhouse gas emissions below 1990 levels – with 1990 a particularly favourable benchmark for these two countries.

At the Rio Earth Summit in 1992, LDCs insisted that affluent nations ought to bear the full burden of this undertaking, since affluent nations, after so many decades of industrial development, were more responsible for existing build-ups of greenhouse gases and better able to bear the cost of reducing new emissions. The LDCs held to this position right up to the 1997 conference in Kyoto which sought to spell out specific national commitments for emission reductions.

By then, however, Britain and Germany had persuaded other EU countries to accept a common stance, by which the EU as a whole would pledge to reduce emissions by as much as 15 per cent while individual EU states could have different targets consistent with this overall result. EU negotiators could not persuade other countries to accept an undifferentiated national commitment to match the EU aggregate and LDCs remained unyielding in their opposition to any reduction commitments. So it was agreed at Kyoto that only a select list of developed countries would commit to specific reductions, varying somewhat from country to country (and all below the EU proposal for 15 per cent cutbacks). For the rest of the world, the Kyoto conference simply agreed, in very vague terms, that the initial efforts of the developed countries would be an example for others to follow at a later period.

In the meantime, the Kyoto Protocol does offer an incentive for LDCs to cooperate. It allows countries that are pledged to make reductions to satisfy some portion of their obligation with assistance programmes that reduce emissions in poor countries (or increase the forest lands there that might act as 'carbon sinks' to draw carbon-dioxide out of the atmosphere and into plants and soil). Such arrangements may give incentives to poor countries to endorse the general doctrine that global warming is a serious problem, requiring serious reductions in emissions. But if it is a serious problem, projected growth in industrial development in LDCs is very likely to cancel any reductions achieved in the affluent countries. By 2010 or 2015, LDCs will probably account for more than half of global emissions. At which point, especially if affluent nations have made sacrifices in the meantime, there are likely to be strong pressures for LDCs to 'do their part'. The obvious way of forcing such cooperation – or penalising a refusal to cooperate – would be trade sanctions.

The supposed justification for such coercion, the underlying threat to the global climate, now seems to have been much exaggerated by environmental advocates. Evidence from satellite monitoring over the past two decades finds little evidence of warming. The UN's own expert panels have quietly scaled back warming projections in each successive report over the past decade, and initial fears of a sudden, catastrophic rise in sea levels from melting polar ice have now been largely discounted by climate scientists.[28]

---

[28] The UN's own Intergovernmental Panel on Climate Change estimated a warming of 4.5 degrees (Fahrenheit) over the next century could raise sea levels by as much as 1 to 3 feet by 2100 – which should not, in itself, be catastrophic, with a century

Even if there is a warming trend, on the other hand, the countries most able to cope with it will be those with the most developed and diversified economies. The least developed countries – those with large populations dependent on subsistence agriculture – would certainly be most exposed to peril, if a global warming trend alters accustomed weather patterns or increases the frequency and intensity of hurricanes. But it hardly follows from this possibility that strict energy controls should now be enacted for the benefit of undeveloped countries. The more prudent response might well be to encourage poor countries to develop their economies as fast as they can right now – so they will be better equipped to deal with climate challenges a century from now – rather than restricting their growth with controls on energy use while they are still desperately poor.[29]

While there may be serious problems down the road, it may still be true that not enough countries can be induced to cooperate on a sufficiently large scale to make any serious difference. Already, the United States Senate has insisted it will not ratify the treaty unless all countries make some commitment to emissions reductions. Getting a solid commitment from the United States will be much easier than getting reliable commitments from China, India, Indonesia and other giants of the developing world.

Yet a new meeting of the parties in Buenos Aires, in November 1998, ended without any new commitments from LDCs, neither was there any acknowledgement that the programme was on the edge of collapse. On the contrary, the Buenos Aires conference called for a new global environmental authority to supervise trading between countries in emission rights. The weakening of the underlying science and policy rationales seems to have no effect on the forward momentum of this undertaking.

d) Into the Soil: Biosafety and POPS

Looking back at these experiences, one might think there was much reason for discouragement about the prospects for international environmental cooperation. In fact, other international agencies have been working to develop new programmes with novel reach and high ambition. Like other programmes, these ventures centre on concerns of special interest to western environmentalists – and threaten unhappy

---

of lead time to prepare the necessary dikes and levees. But it is most uncertain that warming will lead to a rise in sea levels, since it may encourage precipitation in the polar regions, locking more water in snow and insulating polar ice. Some climate experts accordingly predict that a general warming trend might even produce a slight drop in sea-levels. David Schneider, 'The Rising Seas,' *Scientific American*, March 1997, pp. 112-17. Even if a warming trend does have significant negative effects, it may also confer substantial off-setting benefits, from longer growing seasons, reduced heating costs and so on. Thomas Gale Moore, *Climate of Fear* (Washington, D.C.: Cato Institute, 1998) offers a detailed and extensively documented survey of the plausible economic gains from climate change along with reasons for doubting that climate change, on the scale now envisaged, would wreak terrible consequences.

[29] This point is lucidly developed by Thomas C. Schelling, *Costs and Benefits of Greenhouse Gas Reduction* (Washington, D.C.: AEI Press, 1998): 'Even for the grandchildren of those now in India, China, Indonesia and other developing countries, putting a lot of resources into slowing climate change and nothing into their own accelerated development may be the wrong way to go. ... If today we had foreign aid to divide between Bangladesh and Singapore, who would give any to Singapore? But if many developing countries in fifty or seventy-five years will be close to Singapore's level of development now, then it seems backwards to avoid promoting economic development around the world today and focusing on slowing down climate change because of the good it will do for future generations'. (p. 16)

consequences for less developed countries.

The Biodiversity Convention, launched at the 1992 Rio Summit, offers a very broad, general framework for cooperation in protecting threatened eco-systems to preserve specialised flora and fauna. In return for unspecified measures of cooperation, LDCs were promised unspecified forms of royalty payments for biotechnology developed from species in their own territory. Whatever the general benefits, implementing efforts quickly shifted to a marginal aspect of the treaty of special concern to Europeans – a proposed Biosafety Protocol.

The European Union views biosafety issues rather differently from other western nations. Partly this reflects cultural differences – or the differing strength and influence of environmental advocacy groups in Europe. But as in other fields, the EU's peculiar approach also reflects differing economic policies. In an era of global trade, the EU remains very insistent on protecting small farmers in Europe from overseas competition. Efforts to extend trade liberalisation into the agricultural sector were stymied in the Uruguay Round of GATT negotiations (culminating in the 1994 trade agreements), due primarily to EU opposition, and the EU's special view of agriculture has also been displayed in more specialised regulatory disputes.

So, for example, the EU has imposed a ban on hormone treated beef, insisting such treatments pose a genuine health risk for consumers of the resulting meat. No adverse effects on human health have been observed in North America, Australia or Argentina, where cattle commonly receive hormone treatments to stimulate more rapid growth, but the ban fits neatly into larger EU policies designed to protect small farmers in Europe from overseas competition. A long-running dispute over the EU's policy – pitting the EU against Canada, Australia, the United States and other beef exporters – has occupied the GATT (and then the WTO) for a decade, without reaching any resolution. Formal dispute resolution panels have ruled against the EU position, but EU authorities refuse to alter their policy.[30]

The proposed Biosafety Protocol has given a wider dimension to the conflict,

---

[30] Vogel, *Trading Up*, pp. 154-174 reviews the history of this dispute at considerable length. He notes that two extended inquiries by the European Commission's own Scientific Working Group on this issue advised in the early 1980s that several of the disputed hormone treatments were entirely 'harmless for consumers'; the EC responded by cancelling the Working Group's meetings before it could issue a final report. (155). Vogel concludes that the ban was largely motivated by clamour from environmental groups, by determination to harmonize standards at the level favoured by states with the most stringent standards and by one other consideration: 'The ban was also closely linked to another important [European] Community policy, namely the Common Agricultural Programme. By eliminating hormone use, the EC reduced the productivity of European beef producers and thus the supply of beef. This in turn helped protect the economic interests of small, inefficient cattle producers by raising the price of beef and at the same time reduced the subsidies the Community was required to provide them. The latter had, in fact, become quite substantial; the EC's subsidies to beef farmers had increased by more than 56 per cent between 1980 and 1987. The EC's spending on beef rose almost 25 per cent between 1987 and 1988, just as the issue of hormone use was emerging. At the same time EC beef exports were declining and imports were increasing' (164). US Undersecretary of State Stuart Eizenstat recently complained about the EU's refusal to settle this matter: 'After 10 years and two WTO rulings against it, the EU continues to search for the 'right' scientific evidence to support a political prejudice against beef raised with growth hormones. The EU claims to have 17 new studies under way, yet no one can say who is conducting these studies, how they are being run, what procedures they are following and whether there is any opportunity for public review and comment. It is unreasonable and unfair to have the EU endlessly use the excuse of just one more study that might, this time, find something to justify keeping its trade restrictions in place'. Eizenstat, 'Why we should welcome biotechnology,' *The Financial Times* (London), April 16, 1999, p. 16

23

projecting EU concerns and policies onto the rest of the world. Deliberate hybrid breeding of plants is as old as civilisation. Advances in genetic science have made it possible to develop improved plant species in the laboratory. The United States and other western countries have begun to make extensive use of bioengineering. By 1998, such genetically modified strains accounted for 25 per cent of the corn crop, 38 per cent of the soy bean crop and 45 per cent of the cotton crop in the United States. Experts predict that 95 per cent of US agriculture will rely on genetically engineered strains by 2010. The technology has the potential to reduce reliance on chemical pesticides while also making crops more resistant to drought, frost and other hazards. It also has much potential for securing major breakthroughs in pharmacology.

Nevertheless several European countries have already instituted blanket bans on genetically engineered crops and the EU has introduced severe labelling requirements on products made from 'living modified organisms' (LMOs). The proposals for a Biosafety Protocol took an extremely encompassing definition of LMOs and threatened to impose very burdensome testing and notification requirements on international shipments of everything from cereals to cardboard boxes (often treated with corn-starch from genetically engineered corn). US biotech analysts denounced the proposals as 'a trade agreement masquerading as an environmental agreement'.[31]

Most less developed countries rallied to the European position, however. Some nations seemed to be influenced by dire predictions of biological catastrophe, should a Frankenstein strain of cereal run wild in their ecosystems. Others may have been moved by the prospect of international assistance – promised in vague terms in the Protocol – for local testing services, but several LDCs were quite explicit in their protectionist concerns, openly articulating what Europeans did not. Vanilla beans, long a chief export of Madagascar and the Comoros Islands, are now 'being made in vats in California,' a representative of Ethiopia warned. What if genetic engineering should undermine the export value of Ethiopia's coffee?[32] So a number of countries insisted that bioengineering companies in the western world should be required to give notice to LDCs when their technical efforts threatened competitive harm to local crops.

Despite the emerging EU-LDC alliance, the Biosafety Protocol ran into trouble. A conference at Cartegena, Columbia, in February of 1999, which was supposed to launch an agreed text, could not come to agreement. The United States, not having ratified the Biodiversity Convention, was relegated to observer status at the conference. The opposition was mounted by Canada, Australia, New Zealand, Argentina, Chile and Uruguay, all with sizeable agricultural export trade that already makes considerable use of bioengineered species. Most observers predict

---

[31] 'Biosafety Protocol could impede biotech trade, analyst warns,' *Pesticide & Toxic Chemical News* (newsletter of Food Chemical News), Nov. 12, 1998, quoting Adrianne Massey, a consultant for the (U.S.-based) Biotechnology Industry Organization.

[32] Frank Bajak, 'Genetic engineering talks mired in rich, poor nations debate,' Associated Press wire report from Bogata, Feb. 16, 1999

that further negotiations will eventually produce a Biosafety Protocol that does have wide acceptance. The only question is how much it will be slanted to the technophobic or protectionist concerns that have animated earlier efforts.

The stakes have been made still greater by a parallel development. At the very time that international negotiations have threatened to choke off the development of new, pest-resistant plant species, Europe imposed a ban on the production of major pesticides. In June 1988, a conference of European nations approved the 'Aarhus Protocols' (after the Danish city where the conference met), phasing out all production of 16 'persistent organic pollutants' (POPs) and imposing production controls on the use of the heavy metals lead, mercury and cadmium. The new treaty was animated by concern that trace elements of these pollutants had been found to drift hundreds of miles from their source, where they might remain in the soil and ultimately enter into plant or animal food sources, posing eventual health threats to human beings.

The Aarhus Protocols were framed as a supplement or implementing measure under the 1979 European Convention on Long-Range Transboundary Air Pollution (to which Canada and the United States are also parties, along with forty nations in Europe). No sooner had Europe decided to commit to this measure than it sought to bring the rest of the world along: a week after the Aarhus Protocols were signed, the United Nations Environment Programme convened a meeting of 92 nations to enact similar controls on a global basis.[33] The implications for LDCs might be more serious than expected as on the list of POPs slated for prohibition were six frequently used pesticides, including DDT. The Aarhus Protocols call for a ban on DDT 'within one year of a consensus that suitable alternatives are available for public health protection from diseases such as malaria and encephalitis'. This seems to leave the decision up to Europe – where malaria and encephalitis are not raging public health problems, and the Aarhus formula does not clearly reckon with costs: 'suitable alternatives' may be developed (and patented) by western chemical manufacturers, but prove much more expensive to use.

The perspective may be different in the developing world. An intensive campaign against pesticides by western environmentalists has already led to declines in funding by western governments for DDT spraying. Under similar lobbying pressure, the UN's Food and Agricultural Organisation and its World Health Organisation have been discouraging DDT use since the mid-1980s.[34] A

---

[33] Janet Raloff, 'Persistent pollutants face global band,' *Science News*, July 4, 1998, p. 6, reporting UNEP conference in Montreal, with representatives of 92 nations, preparing to consider global controls on industrial chemicals and pesticides, including DDT.

[34] Robert Paarlberg, 'Managing Pesticide Use in Developing Countries,' in Peter Haas, Robert O. Keohane and Marc Levy, *Institutions for the Earth: Sources of Effective International Environmental Protection* (Cambridge, Mass: MIT Press 1994), pp. 316-18, attributes the new international policy stance largely to the 'mostly European based' advocacy organizations associated with the Pesticides Action Network – and also to the opportunities created by a collapse of world food prices in the 1980s as a result of which 'images of global shortage were replaced (especially in the minds of rich country agenda-setters) by images of food surplus'. Paarlberg, himself, cautions that the 'serious harm' that can be done by misuse of pesticides must be balanced against the 'good they have done': 'Tens of millions of human lives have been saved and hundreds of millions of citizens have enjoyed improved health, thanks to the use of chemical insecticides – including DDT – against vector-borne diseases such as malaria. Pesticides have also become a valuable key to crop protection. Roughly 30 per cent of

25

recent medical study, noting alarming increases in malaria infection in South America, demonstrates a close correlation between declining use of DDT and increasing rates of malaria. All countries in the study show increasing malaria rates along with decreasing use of DDT, while Ecuador, which has maintained preventive spraying with DDT, has reported continual declines in malarial infections. The study concludes: 'We are now facing the unprecedented event of eliminating, without meaningful debate, the most cost-effective chemical we have for the prevention of malaria. The health of hundreds of millions of persons in malaria-endemic countries should be given greater consideration before proceeding with the present course of action'.[35]

e) New Frontiers: WHO to WEO

It may be selfish for Europeans to worry more about speculative carcinogenic effects of persistent organic pollutants in their own territory, than about massive increases in malaria in Third World countries. But there is at least some undeniable logic in the concern that pollutants in one part of the world can drift into the territories of other countries. What is striking is the degree to which international regulatory proposals have begun to move from targeting physical entities that do move across national boundaries, to shared agendas based on little more than the movement of ideas –or tastes. Here again, the policy inclinations of the European Union have been projected onto the wider world.

A striking example is the World Health Organisation's effort, beginning in the early 1990s, to mobilise opposition to tobacco use. The health hazards of tobacco use were certainly well known by then, but even those who worry about the dangers of second-hand smoke do not seriously contend that cigarette smoke from one country can drift across the border and victimise unsuspecting citizens of a neighbouring country. The EU had already decided that coordinated action was required, however and promulgated an EU directive imposing a total ban on tobacco advertising in all EU states. Soon after, the WHO began organising its Action Plan for a Tobacco Free Europe.

This was deemed too modest an objective for a *World* Health Organisation. Since 1996, the organisation has been at work on an International Framework Convention on Tobacco Control. Following the pattern of environmental regulatory measures, the initial framework convention is projected to start with general principles and then work its way to serious policy standards in subsequent protocols. WHO has already announced that the initial convention will stake out jurisdiction over pricing and taxing policies to reduce incentives for smuggling of

---

the world's food supply is currently being lost due to pests, plant disease and rodents and an *additional* 30 percent might be lost were it not for the use of chemical pesticides. In the tropical countries of the developing world, where pests that attack plants are especially abundant and where hundreds of millions of poor rural citizens depend upon farming for employment as well as for their food supply, crop protection by chemical pesticides is frequently a matter of life or death'.

[35] Donald R. Roberts, Larry L. Laughlin, Paul Hsheih and Llewellyn J. Legters, Uniformed Services University of the Health Sciences (Bethesda, Maryland, U.S.A.), 'DDT, Global Strategies and a Malaria Control Crisis in South America,' *Emerging Infectious Diseases* **3(3)**, 1997 (US Centers for Disease Control)

cigarettes between countries with differing policies.

The framework convention may also assert international control over advertising, since 'restrictions on tobacco advertising in one country can be undermined by advertising spillover from other countries'.[36] Since illegal drugs manage to find vast markets with no advertising at all, it is not obvious that 'advertising spillovers' are actually a major cause of smoking, but WHO is determined to take a strong stand. Dr Gro Harlem Brundtland, the current Director-General of the WHO, recently explained that 'Smoking is a communicated disease. The allure of smoking is communicated through advertising and peer pressure'.[37] It will be interesting to see what international measures WHO can devise to counter the influence of peer pressure.

In fact, the peer pressure of most interest to WHO appears to be that between governments: 'In practice, only a few [WHO] member states have actually implemented comprehensive tobacco control measures. The planning, scheduling and international information-sharing that would accompany the development of an international convention would facilitate and encourage member states to strengthen their own national tobacco control policies'.[38] In other words, if national governments find it too risky to undertake controversial policies on their own, they may be emboldened to do so in the context of an international programme.

If transnational peer pressure is enough to justify international control policies for tobacco, a lot of other products and practices would seem to qualify for such sharing among nations. Excessive alcohol use is also a major threat to health, along with excessive consumption of high fat foods and inadequate exercise – from such indulgences as excessive reliance on automobiles in some countries. Should the UN promote international regulatory standards to tame these problems, as well?

As a matter of fact, Dr Gro Harlem Brundtland, the current director of the WHO, urged a much wider agenda of international controls in the earlier phases of her career. In the early 1980s, when she was Prime Minister of Norway (and head of the Norwegian Labour Party), she headed a UN Commission on Environment and Development. The 1987 report of this commission (known as the Brundtland Report) stressed that the goal of 'sustainable development' would require cut-backs on consumption patterns that made 'unsustainable demands on the world's finite resources'. It urged such measures as international taxes on the consumption of luxury goods and restraints on energy use.[39] The Brundtland Report (and Dr Brundtland, herself) then played an important role in mobilising support for the 1992 Rio Summit, at which the Framework Convention on Climate Change was adopted.

The themes of the Brundtland Report have since been echoed by advocates of stronger action on climate change. After all, if developing countries now seek to

---

[36] World Health Organisation (Geneva), Fact Sheet No. 160 (May 1998)

[37] Address to the Woodrow Wilson Center, Washington, D.C., September 22, 1998

[38] WHO Fact Sheet 160

[39] World Commission on Environment and Development, *Our Common Future* (Oxford: Oxford University Press, 1987), pp. 341-42

attain western standards of consumption for their vast populations, the resulting surge of industrial activity will place impossible demands on the global environment – at least as some environmental analysts see things. So, for example, on the eve of the Kyoto conference, the Executive Secretary to the Secretariat for the climate change negotiations, observed that 'the present consumption patterns of the rich cannot be generalised globally without unimagined consequences for resource management and environmental security. So it is necessary to bring about sensible changes in those patterns, through education and incentives ... technical standards and fiscal measures that stimulate ... change in consumption habits'.[40]

For now, Brundtland's WHO is focusing on tobacco smoke rather than greenhouse gases, but WHO insists that its efforts at tobacco control must lay the ground for a wider system of controls: 'Tobacco use is a major public health problem, but most of the solutions are to be found outside the health sector, by addressing issues of agriculture, trade, taxation, advertising, package labelling, personnel management and many others'. WHO is therefore cooperating with the UNCTAD and 'seeking the cooperation of other parts of the UN system in the development and operation of a framework convention'.[41] WHO notes with approval the assurance of World Bank President James Wolfensohn that the Bank is 'stepping up our activities on tobacco control – particularly concerning tobacco taxation policies'.[42]

At the same time as it is stepping up to tobacco control, the World Bank has been involving itself with climate change and other concerns. For the Bank, it is the answer to a serious political problem. By the mid-1980s, the World Bank was coming under sharp attack from environmentalists who warned that the Bank's funding of dams and other mega-projects posed a threat to the environment in less developed countries. The Bank responded by promising reforms to ensure that new projects would be environmentally sound. It established new guidelines and internal review procedures to monitor the environmental impact of Bank-funded projects or proposed projects. The Bank also began to make sizeable payments to environmental groups for assistance in such reviews.

Soon, however, governments in recipient countries began to protest excessively intrusive conditions on World Bank funding. In the fall of 1989, German and French representatives to the World Bank proposed a response: a separate Global Environmental Facility (GEF) to make special grants for environmental improvements in poor countries. The new institution was soon funded from major donors of the World Bank. As with the Bank itself, the bylaws of the new GEF leave it under the control of the major donors – of which EU countries are (together) the largest, followed by the US and Japan. So GEF follows the priorities of western governments and responds, to some degree, to the pressures of western environmentalists. Most recently it has been giving emphasis

---

[40] *UN Climate Change Bulletin*, No. 14, 2d Qtr, 1997
[41] WHO Fact Sheet 160
[42] reported on WHO 'Tobacco Free Initiative' website (http: www.who.int/toh/TFI/brundtland.htm)

to projects that promise to reduce greenhouse gas emissions – by converting from cheaper local fuels (such as coal) to less smoky alternatives, often supplied by western energy companies. While the World Bank had poured over $11 billion into environmental projects in less developed countries by 1997, it had carefully ladled over $300 million into programmes operated in partnership with western environmental groups.[43]

Will the GEF continue to operate on its own agenda? Will it be formally merged or at least directly coordinated with the new standard-setting agency proposed at the Buenos Aires conference? That may be only the beginning. There have recently been proposals to establish a larger umbrella organisation, the World Environmental Organisation (WEO), which would take responsibility for all the multilateral environmental agreements that the WTO cannot accommodate.[44] The GEF would presumably operate in close collaboration with the WEO, too.

It is curious and revealing that proposals for new organisations continue to be advanced, even though the United Nations has had a separate agency, supposed to have generalised responsibility for the global environment. The UN Environment Programme (UNEP) was established after the first Earth Summit in Stockholm, Sweden in 1972 and, like most UN agencies, remains ultimately accountable to the UN General Assembly, where each UN member state has an equal vote. With its headquarters in remote Nairobi, Kenya and its limited funding from the UN general budget, UNEP has proved to be a rather marginal and ineffectual player in international negotiations. It was a 'contributor' in the negotiations on ozone depletion and climate change and other ventures, but was never in a position to determine the main lines of negotiation, having no real resources of its own to deploy.

What makes the GEF different is that it is controlled by the small group of western countries that are its principal donors. What makes the WTO different is that, though it nominally operates on a system of equal voting, the major trading nations of the developed world have very disproportionate influence, because they can always ignore the WTO and make their own agreements among themselves: for most countries, the prize in WTO negotiations is access to the markets of western nations, not voting rights in the WTO, per se. So a World Environment Organisation, if it operates in parallel with the WTO and the GEF, will be

---

[43] James M. Sheehan, *Global Greens, Inside the International Environmental Establishment* (Washington, D.C.: Capital Research Center, 1998), p. 155 (breakdown of GEF grants) and pp. 143-54 on the political cross-currents leading to the establishment of the GEF. The GEF has clearly succeeded in buying political support for the Bank among green constituencies: while environmentalists had loudly condemned the Bank for supporting environmentally-damaging projects, they rallied to the Bank's support in 1995, when congressional Republicans (then, newly in the majority) cited past environmental criticism to justify their own (ultimately unsuccessful) effort to reduce US contributions to the Bank.

[44] This proposal seems to have received its first important endorsement in a report by German Green MEP Wolfgang Kreissl-Doerfler, adopted by the European Parliament on November 12, 1996. ('Monitoring Multilateral Environmental Agreements,' *Europe Environment*, No. 488, Nov. 19, 1996). Among other things, the European Parliament also urged that the new organization monitor greenhouse emissions used in the production of goods, so that they could be subject to appropriate punitive duties before being imported into Europe. The Parliament had earlier endorsed a similar proposal for a new international-level 'competition regime requiring international firms to conduct trade in an environmentally friendly manner'. ('European Parliament Adopts Report on Trade and Environment,' *Europe Environment*, No. 478, May 31, 1996)

dominated by the rich nations of the developed world.

Whatever the ultimate organisational configurations, the trend does seem to be toward greater centralisation of environmental programmes. The new power centres are almost certain to give more leverage to the western governments that are most supportive of these programmes and provide the resources and incentives for LDC cooperation with these programmes. EU countries have been the most dedicated to this trend and probably have the strength to maintain its momentum, barring resolute opposition from the US (which seems unlikely). The question for the future is how LDCs will respond to this gathering momentum.

Part III: Three Possible Futures

Trying to chart the future is always hazardous, most especially when one tries to extrapolate from relatively recent, amorphous trends, but given the number and scale of the ventures already underway, it is no longer sensible to think of them as a isolated, disconnected episodes. Clearly, they are different facets of a larger trend in international affairs. Enthusiasts of 'global governance' see these different projects as building blocks of a new world. What kind of world will it be?

In general terms, we can speculate about three different trajectories, with very different consequences. One possibility is that, in looking back from the mid-21st Century, we will see that the current trend ultimately amounted to little more than a 'loud-sounding nothing,' as Castlereagh called Czar Alexander's Holy Alliance. Later generations may observe a mix of idealism, cynicism and delusion that finally led nowhere – like the Hague Peace conferences in the decade before the First World War. The second possibility is that these different trends will finally come together into some sort of 'sustainable development'. The system that emerges may not satisfy visionaries but might prove sufficiently supple and sufficiently acceptable to governments to give substantial, enduring direction to national policies and practices. Yet a third possibility is that the current trend does indeed develop enough momentum to become a serious factor in world affairs– and prove to be a dangerously polarising or divisive force in the world, exacerbating tensions which the new schemes are quite unable to master. Each of these possibilities deserves separate consideration.

The first possibility – a fading into irrelevance – is a well-charted path. We now tend to forget the utopian hopes even quite sober people had for the United Nations in 1945. So, for example, the Charter of the United Nations made provision for a Military Staff Committee which would advise the Security Council on the deployment of a pre-established UN air force, which would be available at any time for immediate UN action to combat aggression or threats to peace.[45] Today it reads like a fantasy out of H.G. Wells. The Charter has not been amended

---

[45] Article 45 of the UN Charter: 'In order to enable the United Nations to take urgent military measures, Members shall hold immediately available national air-force contingents for combined international enforcement action ... by the Security Council with the assistance of the Military Staff Committee'. The Cold War prevented the establishment of a Military Staff Committee in the early years of the UN, but even the ending of the Cold War was not sufficient to breath life into this provision in the 1990s.

but provisions of this sort have long been forgotten.

Perhaps the more instructive analogy is with UN human rights conventions. The UN has sponsored nearly a dozen major human rights treaties over the past half century. By now, almost all countries pay lip service to international human rights agreements. Some advocacy groups enhance their own rhetorical leverage in domestic disputes by invoking useful phrases from UN human rights conventions. Many governments do take some trouble to bring their policies into conformity with standards prescribed in these conventions, but these are usually the same western states that were most active in the drafting of the conventions to begin with.

The fact remains that there is no real penalty for non-compliance with UN human rights conventions.[46] Reports from UN monitors or committees cannot force any government to do anything it does not want to do and other governments feel no obligation to see that particular provisions will really be respected by delinquent states. Soon after China ratified the Covenant on Civil and Political Rights, it began cracking down on dissidents who had the audacity to circulate its text. Neither the UN Human Rights Commission nor any of the member states of the UN expressed great concern.

We might very well see a similar pattern develop in relation to environmental treaties. There is already much evidence to support this projection. China, for example, having signed the Convention on International Trade in Endangered Species in the early 1980s, was recently found to be using government funds to subsidise local ventures aimed at gathering listed species for smuggling abroad.[47] Most LDCs have failed to keep abreast of their obligations to phase out CFCs under the ozone agreements: CFC use has more than doubled in the developing world since the Montreal Protocol went into effect, while production has tripled in China and climbed nearly 9-fold in India.[48] If poor countries do sign onto commitments to reduce greenhouse gas emissions, they are not likely to be very careful about enforcing or complying with such commitments. It may turn out that, the more the global environmental agreements are shown to have little practical effect in poor countries, the more they come to be viewed by affluent western countries, as marginal or symbolic ventures, akin to past human rights accords. Environmental

---

[46] The European Convention on Human Rights (which predates all UN conventions) has much stronger enforcement mechanisms. Rulings of the European Court of Human Rights are not treated dismissively by European governments. And they now have added force, because they can be invoked (as legal precedents) against EU states by the European Court of Justice. But the precise question here is whether European experience can be readily extended to the rest of the world. In the field of human rights, the answer (for now, at least) seems to be that it cannot.

[47] Michael Oksenberg and Elizabeth Economy, *China's Accession to and Implementation of International Environmental Accords, 1978-95* (Stanford University: Asia/Pacific Research Center, 1998), pp. 12-13. In 1992, China submitted a proposal for GEF funding for CITES enforcement, with a 'bid for every province to have its own breeding facilities for tigers in order to generate bones for traditional medicine'. Meanwhile, the Chinese central government 'itself has participated in illegal trade in endangered species. ... In addition, the People's Liberation Army has been implicated in protecting the smugglers of tiger bone and rhino horn. ... Compliance with CITES appears to have been hampered by the interest of ministries in the potential monetary rewards that could be realized both from overt non-compliance and abuse of foreign funds'.

[48] Sebastian Oberthur, Production and Consumption of Ozone Depleting Substances, 1986-1995 (Berlin: Ecologic Centre for International and Environmental Research, 1997), pp. 35, 30.

31

treaties will, in the same way, testify to the world's hopes and ideals but not greatly constrain its actual conduct.

This is a plausible scenario, but it may be the least likely of the three. That is partly because western electorates do seem increasingly open to the view that environmental policies in other continents can affect their own well-being, whereas human suffering in Tibet or Rwanda is a remote abstraction. Most of the current crop of global environmental concerns may prove to be wildly exaggerated, even neurotic, but there is already a well-developed infrastructure of advocacy groups eager to promote and direct these concerns, as certain doctors cater to wealthy hypochondriacs. More importantly, international environmental agreements can enlist powerful business constituencies, which see advantage in rules that protect particular market niches, suppress certain forms of competition or otherwise channel or distort market flows to their advantage. Recent experience suggests that Green activists have learned to work quite well with such business constituencies.

So the second trajectory may be more likely. Call it global projection of the European Union. Like the EU, it will find ways to nurture its own non-governmental constituencies, which can advocate and dramatise new issues and concerns, freed from the limitations of official bureaucracies or elected governments. Like the EU, it will find ways to link the calculations of business executives and economic ministers with the enthusiasms of advocacy groups. Similarly, it will find ways to provide side payments to recalcitrant, poorer states, to sweeten the prospect of submission to the standards most favoured by the wealthier states. All these elements are already in play and can be readily expanded and refined.

It is true, of course, that the European Union could not impose such policies if other western countries were firmly opposed to them, but the United States has more often been hesitant and aloof, rather than firm in its opposition. Often enough, the US has been a ready collaborator with EU initiatives. There is a sizeable environmental movement in the United States and business interests can see their own advantage in certain kinds of agreements. Both NAFTA and the WTO have many critics in the US Congress and few politicians will commit themselves to a resolute defence of free trade, when appealing slogans like 'global environment' or 'international cooperation' are set against it.

Moreover, foreign policy elites in the United States are accustomed to thinking of America as a leader in international negotiations; they are uncomfortable when the US seems to retreat to the role of grumbling critic on the side-lines. Despite contrary advice from his top domestic advisers, for example, President Bush felt obliged to attend the Earth Summit at Rio to prove that the United States was taking its rightful place in the great new ventures being launched there. American leaders will always be tempted to think they have won a victory by getting the EU to temper its ambitions, without forcing a fundamental change of course. This is what happened, after all, in the ozone and climate change negotiations.

If the United States joins in any great undertaking with the EU, smaller western countries – like Canada and Australia – cannot be expected to block their forward momentum. Smaller countries always fear standing outside the 'international consensus': such defiant postures risk offending allies and partners without forcing any change in their policies. The incentives of such countries are to endorse the general programme and then try to bargain for particular concessions to their own circumstances when it comes time to hammer out the details – as Australia did at Kyoto.

The general point is clear enough: small countries do not want to be seen as isolated or 'outside'. Just this psychology has been very crucial to the forward momentum of European integration – on terms most acceptable to Germany and other dominant states: the more powerful the EU becomes, the more determined the smaller countries are to hang on to their places within it, swallowing whatever policy doubts or conflicting interests they may have in the interest of greater unity.

Bringing less developed countries along may be much more difficult since China, India, Brazil and Indonesia, for example, are not small countries. They may be induced to cooperate with a wider range of environmental regulatory schemes, but it would certainly be much easier to secure such cooperation if all the different global environmental initiatives were drawn together and linked with the WTO's trade rules. This may yet happen. The Director-General of the WTO, Renato Ruggiero, has recently proposed the creation of a World Environment Organisation, as a counterpart to the WTO.[49] The idea has enthusiastic support from some environmental advocates. Dr Ruggiero's notion seems to be that a WEO would remove environmental issues from the WTO itself. Some environmentalists hope that a new umbrella organisation for environmental programmes could evolve into a serious counterweight to the WTO, a vehicle for forcing the WTO to mesh environmental standards – and provisions for trade sanctions – with the rules of the trading system.

Bringing diverse programmes under the same organisational umbrella could encourage log-rolling between programmes – as the successive rounds in trade negotiations already proceed by horse trading between major trading nations (or trading blocs) on different issues, with differing levels of interest or priority for different participants. A more unified system might also strengthen the moral and material incentives for states to go along with particular standards or proposals they do not really like, lest they become isolated or marginalised in negotiations that matter more to them on other subjects – in a scheme where a significant range of issues are pursued under the same umbrella organisation.

As the WTO now has a relatively formalised system for arbitrating trade disputes, we may well see the development of more formalised mechanisms for arbitrating or assessing complaints of non-compliance with environmental norms.

---

[49] Frances Williams, 'Washington Urges WTO to be More Responsive to Ecological Concerns,' *The Financial Times* (London), March 16, 1999, p. 8, reporting that Director Ruggiero had 'repeated his call for a more powerful World Environment Organisation with which the WTO could deal on an equal basis'.

In any case, a more centralised system would likely develop the staffing and institutional resources (with its own network of scientific and economic advisers) to become a bureaucracy with its own agenda rather than a mere host for conferences. In other words, we might see the advent of an international counterpart to the European Commission, operating in a system that is far more loosely linked than the European Union but bears obvious family resemblance.

But if this vision is plausible and quite attractive to many advocacy groups, it carries with it the seeds of the third possibility – an exacerbation of international tensions. The momentum of existing programmes and proposals is already effacing any clear distinction between international and domestic concerns – just as the EU has broken down any clear principle or boundary between what is properly a matter for European-wide policy and what must be left to national governments to resolve for themselves. Less developed countries are eager for international assistance but also jealous of international interference. The more ambitious international regulation becomes, in terms of carrying forward costly and intrusive programmes, the more it is likely to provoke fear and resentment. The details of any particular policy may be too eye-glazingly technical to engage the mass public on any particular dispute, but the image and symbolism of international coercion may rankle at some level and be ready fodder for demagogic campaigns.

This has already been the experience with the IMF and the World Bank. In many parts of the world, these Washington-based institutions now provoke the sort of paranoia and resentment once reserved for the CIA, even though the western governments which largely control these international lending institutions do not insist that troubled countries accept their assistance. Governments often disregard local political protests against disagreeable conditions attached to the loans, because they are desperately in need of new loans.

The calculus of costs and benefits may look rather different in relation to cooperating with international environmental programmes. It is all too easy to imagine China or India or Brazil organising a broad coalition of states to resist the aims or efforts of a World Environmental Organisation. If existing trends continue, they may have considerable grounds to characterise the WEO (and with it, perhaps, the WTO) as a tool of the rich countries which does more harm than good to the developing world.

To the extent that a WEO has worked out a system for meshing its standards with WTO trading privileges, it is easy to imagine bitter disputes in one area spilling over to disrupt or divide the trading system. Protectionist forces in western countries might well be pleased to find new opportunities for imposing trade sanctions. In a more divided and turbulent world, leaders of developing nations might also think it advantageous to harp on peripheral environmental disputes, as a means of challenging irksome disciplines of the trading system.[50] Such challenges

---

[50] Governments of LDCs have not yet been very public about their grievances but NGOs from such countries are already preparing local opinion for defiant stances. So, for example, the Harare Caucus of African NGOs, meeting in Isiolo, Kenya on November 5, 1998, issued the following warning: 'There is a shift from conservational to economic management of the

might prove self-destructive or self-defeating but many governments are tempted to play a defiant or demagogic role, challenging accepted international norms even when they have little hope of replacing them with better alternatives.

Some observers worry that the EU has become too ambitious in its reach to preserve long-term harmony among the member states. Whether that is so or not, global programmes must encompass a much wider range of nations, most of which have far less obvious and immediate incentives to pull together in common efforts. Piling new aims and new powers onto international institutions can as easily divide the world as unite it. The more some of the world is drawn together in a green vision, the more other countries may recoil and rebel. Trying to secure a greener world might prove, in the end, a recipe for a much more restless and embittered world.

It remains true, of course, that global trade in itself creates vast disruption and dislocation, along with new opportunities for improved efficiency and enhanced growth. Compared to the resentments stirred by global trade, the extra burdens of environmental controls may seem a relatively secondary matter, however trade-related disruptions are the result of impersonal market forces. It is not as easy to stir demagogic protests against impersonal market forces as against an identifiable institution.

Partly for this reason, economic liberalisation of domestic markets has often proved to have a political tranquillising effect. There was, for example, less class-based strife in Britain by the late 1980s than there had been a decade earlier. Rising prosperity was part of the reason. Perhaps equally important, however, was a new political reality: a government which had disclaimed broader responsibilities for assuring economic equity could not be so easily blamed for localised discontents.

Most countries of the European Union, however, have not liberalised labour markets to the same extent as Britain. Governments in most European countries therefore remain highly vulnerable to political protests regarding short-term economic trends and localised economic effects. A Europe that is sceptical of liberal policy at home is naturally inclined to promote the idea that global markets must be supplemented by the guiding hand of international institutions.

This tendency raises the central danger in spreading the EU governing style to the wider world. If prominent international institutions come to take responsibility for environment and development, poor countries will be tempted to place the blame for their developmental problems on these same international institutions. Perhaps newly empowered global authorities will be nimble enough to cope with the ensuing protests, but Europeans provoked a great deal of rage and resentment in earlier times, when they tried to take responsibility for development in Africa and Asia. There is no obvious reason to trust that future ventures will have happier

---

environment evidenced by the trend toward environmental imperialism by the north, where the largest environmental culprits are found. Environmental protection standards are used as nontariff barriers to southern products or as excuses to back out of large development projects in the south, while northern [corporations] remain untouched. This amounts to a cosmetic adoption of environmental protection standards by [international financial institutions], undermining indigenous peoples' movements for their own forms of environmental management'.

results, and more may be at stake than a series of ill-conceived environmental programmes.

GLOBAL GREENS

Inside the International Environmental Establishment

James M. Sheehan

Addressing a black tie dinner of the United Nations Association in September 1997, media magnate Ted Turner shocked the world with the announcement that he would contribute $1 billion to the United Nations. Turner's gift – roughly the size of the UN's annual operating budget – will be used to fund normal activities of the international organisation. But it comes with politically correct strings attached. The billionaire founder of CNN and vice-chairman of Time Warner is a strident advocate of environmentalist causes and he wants the UN to use his money to promote his agenda. 'I've wanted for some time to do something for the United Nations because I think it's the organisation with the greatest reach and potential for doing good in the post-Cold War world, for helping children and the environment and promoting peace,' he said.

Turner's backing is an enormous windfall for an organisation that is nearly bankrupt. Because the UN has failed to undertake needed management reforms, the US Congress cut voluntary US government contributions that were roughly equivalent to the amount of the gift. Consequently, private philanthropy is relieving pressure on UN officials to make changes demanded by Congress. Turner insists that his money not be used for administrative expenses. But UN officials are permitted to take funds from the programme agencies he is supporting and redirect them to New York headquarters, site of the organisation's most entrenched and top-heavy bureaucracy. They understand that money is fungible.

Turner's money will be funnelled through international agencies such as the UN Population Fund, the World Health Organisation and the UN Environment Programme. But non-governmental organisations, or NGOs, will be central in planning and implementing his agenda. Turner understands the crucial role they play and he has made sure that his UN Foundation guarantees their continued power and influence.

What are NGOs and why do they figure so prominently in the international environmental establishment?

The NGO emerged in the early 1990s as a prominent new force in international affairs. Before the Cold War's end, foreign policy was mainly the domain of government officials. Western industrial powers concerned themselves with international security and arms control negotiations and diplomacy was handled mainly through direct bilateral contacts. Environmental issues had little standing on the world stage and environmental groups focused almost exclusively on domestic issues and the actions of national and local governments.

Since the 1992 Earth Summit in Rio de Janeiro, the environmental credo

'Think globally, act locally' has been permanently altered. Not only do greens act locally, they're eager to act globally as well. Non-governmental advocacy groups are involved in international efforts to plan global economic development, regulate science and technology, restrict population growth and intervene in social policymaking. Even in the traditional areas of foreign and defence policy, environmental groups push their issues to the forefront. An all-encompassing green ideology is now an integral part of the vocabulary of our policymakers.

NGOs have played a critical role in transforming the international political agenda. They are both critics and advisers of governments. They have joined national governments, central banks and international agencies as institutions authorised to define the world's problems and propose policy fixes. From the calling of United Nations conferences to the negotiation of international treaties, NGOs today exert a profound influence on international affairs.

The United Nations defines an NGO as 'any non-profit, voluntary citizens' group which is organised on a local, national or international level'.[1] This monograph will examine some of the most politically influential NGOs that focus on international environmental questions. It will review the positions they take and it will describe their methods of lobbying governments and international agencies.

It is not easy to narrate the story of international environmental groups. The range of issues they pursue is extensive, yet sources of information about them are few and often self-serving. Still, if we want to understand current international environmental policies we must know more about how these organisations have affected them. This study describes the successes and failures of international environmental NGOs, concentrating on the past half-dozen years when they have been most active. I am hopeful that this chronicle of their activities will help the public and policymakers appreciate the scope of their goals and accomplishments.

Environmental groups are achieving their objectives gradually and largely under a cloak of secrecy. Few people know that non-profit organisations, staffed by professionals, primarily Americans and financed by a mix of private and public funds, exercise real power in the conduct of diplomacy and the creation of international policy. A global environmentalist movement is using international law and the assistance of the United Nations and other international agencies to undermine national self-government, economic freedom and personal liberty. This monograph shines light on the behind-the-scenes efforts of this well-funded and ideologically-driven political force.

---

[1] United Nations Department of Public Information, DPI/1438/Rev.1-07508-October 1995.

1. The New World of the NGO

A giant Tyrannosaurus Rex constructed of junk metal towers over a conference hall in a mid-sized Japanese city. Inside, a small group is fanning out across the building to cover every empty table, door and corridor with propaganda leaflets. Four masked men, disguised as world leaders, play a game of soccer with a large inflatable balloon of the planet. The game is being recorded by several video cameras. Out front, reporters are photographing another group of grim-faced individuals who stand solemnly around three ice carvings of penguins. They are begging the little creatures to forgive mankind for permitting the 'global warming' that is now causing them to melt.

Is this is a theatre of the absurd? No. It is a United Nations conference in Kyoto, Japan, where a very serious treaty to stop global warming is nearing completion. Lawyers and lobbyists employed by well-funded environmental organisations are huddling in a side room with diplomats and dignitaries, crafting a legal document to curtail energy use in industrialised countries. It is a familiar scene for Green activists, who are accredited by the UN to attend the conference as non-governmental organisations (NGOs).

Welcome to the brave new world of the NGO, where full-time activists attend international treaty-making proceedings as UN-accredited representatives of the public. The UN describes its conferences as sites for 'democratic' international governance. But none of the thousands of individuals who participate in these events, save a handful of speech-makers, is elected to public office or authorised to represent UN member governments. Yet by virtue of UN accreditation, members of NGOs are privileged to scold, advise and mingle with the leaders of the world.

Besides participating in UN-sponsored treaty negotiations, NGOs are involved in a wide range of related activities. They design and propose texts for international treaties, conventions and other international law instruments. They monitor governments and private businesses to determine whether they are in compliance with national and international rules. Their attorneys file suit in US and foreign courts against public and private bodies they consider to be out of compliance with law. NGOs sponsor consumer boycotts and launch media campaigns against policies, companies and governments they oppose. Indeed, the most enterprising NGOs help governments enforce environmental legislation that their own lobbyists have helped write in response to 'public' protests their own activists organised!

NGOs assert proudly that they are independent of governments and private industry. They claim to act in the public interest, free of outside pressure and influence and they purport to offer viewpoints that are more objective than the views of private industry. The news media often treats NGOs as unbiased observers.

Yet NGOs usually have a radical political agenda. Most believe that the private sector cannot solve environmental problems and that governments must control economic decision-making to protect the environment. This belief may be quite sincere, but it is also rooted in self-interest. Many NGOs depend on governments for jobs, money and power. They seek out grants and contracts from national governments and international agencies. They also bask in the recognition they receive from public agencies, which adds authority to their pronouncements and brings prestige to their leaders.

A New Kind of Organisation

An estimated 4,000 NGOs worldwide are active in environmental matters.[2] They are not focused exclusively on environmental issues, but include women's associations, consumer groups, farmers cooperatives, human rights organisations, labour unions, private relief charities, policy analysis centres, think tanks and political action groups.[3] Despite this apparent diversity, many NGOs have discovered that 'environmentalism' is a winning concept around which they can mobilise support.

Most of the largest environmental NGOs have always had an international focus and some have offices in several countries.[4] Others have deliberately transformed themselves into international organisations. Friends of the Earth International, for example, is a decentralised confederation of over fifty affiliates. Greenpeace, which is based in Amsterdam, has members in 20 different countries. The Worldwide Fund for Nature (WWF) boasts twenty-eight national affiliates.[5] The World Conservation Union-IUCN is an umbrella organisation of private groups and government agencies that comprises approximately 450 members.[6]

NGOs have a variety of different missions. Some identify themselves as grassroots organisations working in cities, villages, or rural areas in developing countries. Many offer special or technical services to other NGOs by doing field work, raising money, or handling litigation and other legal defence work.[7] Policy research groups such as the World Resources Institute and the Worldwatch Institute publish books and technical reports that identify problems and propose government policy solutions. And there are coalition-building organisations that assemble and represent other organisations to encourage the formation of still more 'grassroots' groups.

---

[2] Gareth Porter and Janet Welsh Brown, *Global Environmental Politics*, 2d edition, (Boulder: Westview Press, 1991, 1996) p. 50.

[3] World Resources Institute, United Nations Environment Programme and United Nations Development Programme, *World Resources 1992-1993: A Guide to the Global Environment*, (New York: Oxford University Press), p. 216.

[4] All major US-based environmental groups pursue international activities. The oldest conservation organisations – the Sierra Club, National Audubon Society and National Wildlife Federation – were created at the turn of the century to address domestic concerns, but in recent years they have developed international departments with expanded agendas. The Environmental Defence Fund and the Natural Resources Defence Council were founded in the 1970s to litigate in US courts and influence executive branch enforcement of environmental regulations. Today, each is active on the international front covering such issues as global warming and ozone depletion. Even the animal rights-oriented Defenders of Wildlife and Humane Society of the United States have gone international. They attempt to influence overseas enforcement of such US policies as the Marine Mammal Protection Act and environmental standards for international trade. (Porter and Brown, p.53.)

[5] Porter and Brown, *Global Environmental Politics*, 1996, p.51.

[6] Thomas Princen and Matthias Finger, *Environmental NGOs in World Politics*, (New York: Routledge, 1994) p. 2.

[7] Ibid.

By far the most important NGO activity is the written word. Books, papers, press conferences and news releases fill the arsenal of many NGOs. Environmental groups have become adept at 'spinning' stories to the news media to persuade the public that global government programmes are essential to its well-being. Ironically, their effectiveness has been enhanced by something that also incites their deepest suspicion – modern technology. Advances in communications allow NGOs to communicate with allies and affiliates all over the world. Fax machines, the Internet, satellite television signals and cellular phones are the international environmental movement's weapons of choice.

A more traditional instrument for gaining attention is what environmentalists call 'direct action' – visible public protests, demonstrations and dramatic stunts. This type of activism can range from peaceful picketing and sit-ins by grassroots activists to the well-timed announcement of boycotts and the filing of lawsuits by organisations sensitive to newspaper deadlines. More extreme forms of direct action involve the provocation of violence. Greenpeace is notorious for piloting small boats into the path of massive warships carrying nuclear weapons. Sea Shepherd, a militant group founded by a radical former member of Greenpeace, specialises in sinking or destroying whaling vessels. Earth First! pioneered the practice of eco-sabotage or 'monkey-wrenching' against forestry and mining sites.[8] Yet even these groups claim a place at the table when public policy is debated.

The role of NGO coalitions deserves particular notice. Acting as front groups, they can sometimes make support for a cause appear stronger than it really is by temporarily gathering disparate groups together under the banner of a common purpose. NGO coalitions also lay claim to legitimacy by unifying around issues that cross international boundaries. For example, the Climate Action Network (CAN) comprises NGOs from twenty-two countries that have allied to lobby for restrictions on energy emissions.9

In recent years NGOs have successfully gained official status as participant-observers at international environmental conventions, conferences and negotiations. While they continue to proclaim their outsider status, NGOs now have the political experience and technical expertise of insiders. With official observer status, they participate in the periodic follow-up meetings to environmental conventions that are known as 'conferences of the parties,' or COPs. COPs are extended negotiations that build on the basic framework created by the initial convention. NGOs help set the agenda of these conferences by making detailed policy proposals or calling for specific actions. They often use COPS as opportunities to promote the revision or amendment of existing treaty obligations.

Particular NGOs have become experts over time on particular sets of negotiations. Greenpeace, for instance, has expertise in the international regulation of hazardous waste. It has dominated the agenda of the Basle Convention on trade

[8] Philip Shabecoff, *A New Name for Peace: International Environmentalism, Sustainable Development and Democracy*, (Hanover, NH: University Press of New England, 1996) p. 73.
[9] Porter and Brown, p.53.

in hazardous waste since the beginning of negotiations in the late 1980s by employing a unique brand of conference participation, report-writing and lobbying. Greenpeace has managed successfully to impose treaty obligations on the countries of the world that are much tougher than many would have preferred. Its political and organisational skills can only be admired.

The NGO community is a vast resource. NGOs have accumulated deep reservoirs of scientific and technical expertise, but they can also muster large groups of demonstrators and issue a blizzard of press releases to give politicians the protective cover of apparent public support. And they can assemble impressive behind-the-scenes lobbying forces. Officials in national and international environment ministries, who are often very sympathetic to their positions, develop close relations with many NGOs. They rely on the strengths of NGO organisations and help them obscure their weaknesses.

Working with the United Nations

Nearly 1,500 organisations are registered with the United Nations Department of Public Information. The Department says it 'helps those NGOs gain access to and disseminate information concerning the spectrum of United Nations priority issues, to enable the public better to understand the aims and objectives of the world Organisation'.[10] Such bland language masks the extraordinary political activism NGOs can take on the UN's behalf. According to UN guidelines, accredited NGOs are expected to use their information programmes to promote public awareness of UN principles and activities. In practice, this means that NGOs engage in intensive lobbying of governments to support UN environmental policies, while fiercely attacking UN critics.

UN officials have come to recognise the importance of NGOs. Former UN Secretary General Boutros Boutros-Ghali has called NGO participation in the international organisation 'a guarantee of the latter's political legitimacy'.[11] The result is a system of mutual support: NGOs promote a policy, the UN enacts it and both benefit. In Rio de Janeiro, NGOs galvanised support for a new global policy of 'sustainable development'; in Cairo they clamoured for worldwide controls over population growth. NGOs publicise these and other activities, boost citizen participation in them and promote favourable reviews of their outcomes. This legitimising role cannot be underestimated. The UN enhances this process by ensuring that NGOs seeking UN accreditation (which is necessary for participation in UN conferences) fulfil a stringent set of criteria; they must:[12]

- Share the ideals of the United Nations;
- Operate solely on a not-for-profit basis;
- Have a demonstrated interest in United Nations issues and proven ability to

---

[10] United Nations Department of Public Information, DPI/1438/Rev.1-07508-October 1995.
[11] Ibid.
[12] Ibid.

reach large or specialised audiences, such as educators, media representatives, policy makers and the business community;

- Have the commitment and means to conduct effective information programmes about United Nations activities through publication of newsletters, bulletins, backgrounders and pamphlets; organisation of conferences, seminars and round tables; and enlisting the cooperation of print and broadcast media.

Most NGOs have consultative status with the UN Economic and Social Council, which is responsible for calling international conferences and preparing draft treaties. As such, NGOs may send observers to public meetings of the Council and its subsidiaries and they are encouraged to submit written comments and proposals pertaining to the Council's work.[13] Subsequent chapters of this study will describe in detail NGO activity in some of the most significant UN conferences in recent years.

NGO Attacks on Business

The environmental activist who helps a friendly government bureaucrat may also threaten the hostile corporate executive. NGOs have honed their political attack skills by targeting multinational corporations with overseas investments and manufacturing operations. One survey of 51 large European corporations found that 90 per cent expected pressure groups to maintain or increase the intensity of their campaigns over the next five years.[14]

This is perhaps not surprising when one considers the objectives of these groups. Greenpeace, for example, makes no secret of its desire to shut down nuclear, oil and whaling companies, as well as to eliminate all synthetic chlorine compounds from the world. According to Greenpeace UK, environmental activism is not meant to analyse problems and propose solutions, but to 'connect the problem to those who are responsible for it and ... hunt them down and eliminate problems'.[15] The following controversies demonstrate the brazenness and ingenuity of NGO demands.

The Campaign against Royal Dutch Shell

In 1995 Greenpeace mounted two successful campaigns against Royal Dutch Shell, which resulted in the company's almost total capitulation to the demands of these environmental extremists.

The first campaign focused on the proposed disposal of an off-shore oil platform, the Brent Spar, in the North Sea. Shell had decided to sink the platform; an option that was cost-effective, would have little environmental impact and had received the backing of the British government. In spite of this, Greenpeace flew activists to the platform, videotaping the assault and sharing its images with the

---

[13] UN brochure, 'Basic Facts About the United Nations,' #E.95.I.31; Press Release ORG/1211/Rev.1.

[14] Control Risks Group Limited, *No Hiding Place: Business and the Politics of Pressure*, July 1997.

[15] *Greenpeace Business*, London, February/March 1996, as quoted in *No Hiding Place: Business and the Politics of Pressure*, p. 12.

media. Their justifications for this action included the baseless claim that the platform contained 5000 tonnes of toxic materials.

While television viewers saw a small band of activists confronting a multinational corporation, the reality was quite different. Greenpeace spent well in excess of $2 million on a sophisticated public relations strategy to coordinate actions to influence public opinion. Militants on Brent Spar used cellular phones and computers to contact other Greenpeace activists, who initiated protests at Shell gas stations across Europe. Shell's scientific and legal arguments defending its decision proved to be no match for the dramatic incident that Greenpeace staged.[16]

The second campaign focused on Shell's activities in Ogoniland, Nigeria. Greenpeace alleged that Shell was responsible for the Nigerian government's execution of political activist Ken Saro-Wiwa, leader of the Ogonis and self-proclaimed environmentalist who was charged with and convicted of inciting murder (the charges were denied by environmental and human rights NGOs). Greenpeace accused Shell of failing to use its influence to curb government abuses and also alleged that the company damaged tribal lands by allowing its pipelines to leak oil.

Shell pointed out that it could hardly intervene in a civil conflict between rival political factions and that any effort to do so would invite attacks on its operations. It had already withdrawn from Saro-Wiwa's home region, Ogoniland, where civil strife created major security problems (amongst other things, militant Ogonis had been damaging Shell's pipelines and then claiming compensation for damage to their land). Shell officials said no private company could be held responsible for the abuses of a foreign power.

In response to these campaigns, Shell has revised its business plans to take into consideration the likely threat of future environmentalist actions. Amongst other things, this has meant spending several million dollars on the consultation process relating to the disposal of the Brent Spar – which will now be converted into a harbour at a cost of around $35million – probably a less environmentally sound option than the initial $7.5million proposed sea disposal.

The Campaign Against Freeport McMoRan

Freeport McMoRan Copper & Gold, Inc. operates the Grasberg mine located in Indonesia's easternmost province of Irian Jaya on the island of New Guinea. It is the largest gold mine in the world. Environmentalists accuse Freeport of violating the human rights of the indigenous people and of degrading the area's rivers and rainforests with its mine waste. They say the New Orleans-based company abets Indonesia's military suppression of a separatist tribal movement in Irian Jaya.

Three organisations waged a campaign against Freeport: 1) the Indonesian Forum for the Environment, also known as Walhi, which is an affiliate of the US-based Friends of the Earth; 2) the Berkeley, California-based International Rivers Network; and 3) Partisans, a single-issue group which opposes Rio Tinto, a

---

[16] *No Hiding Place: Business and the Politics of Pressure*, p. 21.

London-based mining company with a substantial investment in Freeport.[17]

The US Agency for International Development gave Walhi more than $1.3 million for the campaign against Freeport Mcmoran.[18] Walhi used its resources to lobby the US Overseas Private Investment Corporation (OPIC), a federal agency that provides US foreign investments with subsidised risk insurance. In June 1995, International Rivers Network lawyer Lori Udall organised a coalition of NGOs to help Walhi pressurise OPIC into suspending its risk insurance for Freeport's Indonesian investments.[19] The coalition demanded that independent NGO panels be set up to settle land rights disputes and other issues involving Freeport. It accused the company of moral responsibility for the killing of rebels by Indonesia's military.[20] And it organised a picket of the New Orleans home of Freeport's chairman, Jim Bob Moffett; pickets carried placards saying 'Jim-Bob Moffett Kills for Profit'.[21]

Freeport responded by asserting that it had complied with all applicable environmental laws and that an audit by the Dames & Moore consulting firm commended the company's $25 million mine waste management programme. The company also noted that Indonesia's Roman Catholic bishop had cleared it of any moral responsibility for incidents between government troops and rebel factions. Furthermore, the company warned that the proposed NGO panels amounted to a Walhi shadow government that 'would be regarded in Indonesia as a usurpation of provincial and national government authority and responsibility'.[22]

Freeport failed to stem the international uproar created by Walhi and its American allies. OPIC cancelled Freeport's $100 million insurance contract which protected the company's $2.8 billion investments in Irian Jaya against the possibility of expropriation. This was the first time in OPIC's 25-year history that it had withdrawn coverage because of environmentalist objections. Freeport reacted by offering to give $15 million annually to Indonesian NGOs. This was in addition to the $22 million per year it spent on agriculture and land improvement, schools and hospitals, infrastructure spending on a seaport and airport and wages for 7,000 local employees who earned almost twice the average national income. After several months of arbitration OPIC eventually reversed its decision, but only after Freeport had pledged to place another $100 million in a trust fund for Irian Jaya environmental initiatives.[23]

---

[17] 'Moving from Problem Exposing to Problem Solving,' Walhi's Concept Paper to Build the Foundation to Achieve Solution for Environmental and Social Problems of Amungme People Caused by Freeport Mining Operation in Timika, Fakfak District, Irian Jaya, Indonesia, submitted by Wahana Lingkungan Hidup Indonesia (Indonesian Forum for Environment).

[18] Brigid McMenamin, 'Environmental Imperialism,' *Forbes*, May 20, 1996.

[19] The NGO coalition included the Centre for International Environmental Law, Friends of the Earth, Bank Information Centre, National Wildlife Federation, Sierra Club, Environmental Defence Fund and Natural Resources Defence Council.

[20] Letter to James R. Moffett from Lori Udall of International Rivers Network and David Hunter of Centre for International Environmental Law, November 28, 1995.

[21] Alan Gersten, 'Moffett Confronts Strife in Indonesia,' *Journal of Commerce*, June 21, 1996; McMenamin, 'Environmental Imperialism.'

[22] Letter to Lori Udall from Thomas J. Egan, Senior Vice President, Freeport-McMoRan Copper and Gold, Inc., December 8, 1995.

[23] Alan Gersten, 'Coverage Reinstated for Freeport Mine,' *Journal of Commerce*, April 23, 1996.

The Campaign Against Mitsubishi

In 1990, the aggressive direct-action group Rainforest Action Network (RAN) began a campaign against Japan's giant Mitsubishi Corporation, accusing it of degrading tropical rainforests. Eight years later, Mitsubishi Motor Sales and Mitsubishi Electric America agreed to alter their production practices. In a 'Memorandum of Understanding,' the Mitsubishi firms agreed to conduct environmental reviews of their operations and pledged to use more alternative fibres, to phase out tree-based paper and packaging products by 2002 and to use timber only from sources certified as 'sustainable' by organisations such the Forest Stewardship Council.[24]

Mitsubishi also signed a 'Statement of Global Ecological Crisis,' which condemned human activities that harm nature and it promised to fund media advertisements in collaboration with RAN to trumpet the importance of society's transition to 'an ecological economy'. The firms further agreed to fund a 'Forest Community Support Programme' administered by organisations acceptable to RAN, such as Friends of the Earth.

One Mitsubishi pledge signalled something new. The sub-divisions promised to incorporate 'Natural Step' training programmes into their operations. Natural Step, an environmental organisation founded in Sweden in 1989, believes that organisations should adhere to the following principles:

- *Substances from the Earth's crust can not systematically increase in the biosphere.*

- *Substances produced by society can not systematically increase in the biosphere.*

- *The physical basis for the productivity and diversity of nature must not be systematically deteriorated.*

- *In order to meet the previous three system conditions, there must be a fair and efficient use of resources to meet human needs.*[25]

If a company were actually to abide by these bizarre principles, it could not extract fossil fuels, metals or minerals from the earth's crust 'at a rate faster than their re-deposit'. Synthetic substances would be phased out; land use and consumption would be reduced to levels that nature could sustain without human intervention.

What did Mitsubishi get in return for its pledge? For its part, RAN agreed to end its consumer boycott and promised to end its disruptive protest actions at

---

[24] The Forestry Stewardship Council, set up by the WWF is a scheme that certifies 'sustainably produced' timber.
[25] www.emis.com/tns/documents/IntroTNS.htm

Mitsubishi auto shows, car dealerships and electronics stores.[26]

The Shifting Fortunes of International Environmentalism

The history of international environmentalism is a history of ideological commitment and political confrontation. The environmental movement is an outgrowth of America's 1960s counterculture and the radical anti-war movement. It drew inspiration from Rachel Carson's best-selling 1962 work, *Silent Spring* and other works which decry the products and by-products of modern industrial society: chemicals, pesticides, radiation and toxic waste. Many environmental activists are repulsed by modern society and in seeking alternatives to it, they often seem to find in nature forms of spirituality that give their politics the appearance of a pagan cult.[27]

Many environmental groups, such as Greenpeace and the Rainforest Action Network, relish direct confrontation with corporations. But the maturing of the movement in the 1980s and 90s led other groups to prefer the leverage of government regulation. The leaders of environmental groups have become weighty players in international public affairs.

The process began in 1972 with the UN Conference on the Human Environment held in Stockholm, Sweden and chaired by Maurice Strong, a wealthy Canadian industrialist and diplomat, which brought the environmental movement to the attention of the world's policymakers. Indeed, the commitments made at Stockholm prompted 114 governments to create national environmental ministries. Stockholm also produced the UN's own environmental agency, the UN Environment Programme (UNEP), which would be responsible for coordinating international environmental protection. UNEP subsequently convened three environmental conventions: on the international trade in endangered species, on whaling and on ocean dumping.[28]

UNEP's first executive director, Maurice Strong, was in no small measure responsible for the environmentalists' first international success. At Stockholm, environmental advocacy groups held a side conference to supplement the official UN proceeding. Known as the 'Hog Farm,' it served as a forum for activist speeches, protest demonstrations and the issuance of demands on official conference delegates. (This subsequently became standard practice at UN conferences.) When Hog Farm participants insisted that governments impose an international ban on whaling to 'Save the Whale,' Maurice Strong acted quickly. Following the Stockholm conference, he flew to London to a meeting of the International Whaling Convention (IWC) and prevailed on delegates to give the activists what they wanted. To this day, Strong credits the IWC decision to the

---

[26] Rainforest Action Network, 'Landmark Settlement Reached in Long-Running Environmental Boycott of Two Mitsubishi Companies,' press release, www.ran.org/ran/ran_campaigns/mitsubishi/QT/release.html.
[27] See Jonathan H. Adler, *Environmentalism at the Crossroads*, (Washington, DC: Capital Research Centre, 1996).
[28] William K. Stevens, 'Earth Summit Finds the Years of Optimism a Fading Memory,' *New York Times*, June 9, 1992, p. C4.

heavy outside pressure exerted by the NGOs in Stockholm.[29]

But the governments of developing countries did not welcome environmentalist victories of this kind. They planned to utilise their natural resources to try and strengthen their economies and raise living standards and were afraid that the international environmental lobby would stymie their efforts. They resented what they regarded as patronising and colonial environmentalist demands. Over time this attitude hardened and at later UN conferences it would pose a significant challenge to Green ideology.

Third World governments had their own ideology. In 1974, the UN General Assembly passed a resolution calling for a New International Economic Order (NIEO). It envisioned international commodity agreements, projects for North-South wealth redistribution and other global schemes. NIEO was inspired by the ideas of radical Marxist intellectuals and supported by anti-Western politicians who were attracted to theories of centralised economic planning that promised to increase their power.

Many Western political leaders understood that NIEO was an economic disaster for the Third World and a political weapon for the Soviets. But some environmental activists believed they could use it to enact UN environmental policies. For example, the UN Conference on the Law of the Sea, a massive undertaking to establish an international legal regime for the world's oceans, declared the mineral resources under the sea to be the 'common heritage of mankind' and proposed that they be put under UN control and management to create a 'just and equitable economic order'.

Perhaps the most important strand in environmentalist thinking has been that associated with the belief that we are running out of resources. This view owes much to Robert Malthus, whose 1798 'Essay on the Principle of Population' postulated that in the absence of certain checks, such as war, famine and disease, human numbers would increase at a rate faster than the means of supporting them. The modern-day equivalent of Malthus is Paul Ehrlich, who claimed in a 1968 book, 'The Population Bomb,' that as a result of over-population the world would soon exceed its carrying capacity and that by the 1980s millions of people in the developed world would be starving.[30] This neo-Malthusian tract heralded the 'limits to growth' philosophy popularised in the 1970s by such influential groups as the Club of Rome, which called for government control over economic growth, resource use and energy consumption.[31] In 1980 the outgoing Carter administration's *Global 2000 Report to the President* took a similar position.[32]

The predictions of Ehrlich, the Club of Rome and Global 2000 have been annihilated by reality but they were also refuted by the late Julian Simon and

---

[29] Shabecoff, p. 39.
[30] Paul Ehrlich, *The Population Bomb*, (New York: Sierra Club/Ballantine, 1968).
[31] Donella H. Meadows, et al, *The Limits to Growth*, (New York: Universe Books, 1972).
[32] *Global 2000 Report to the President* (Washington, DC: Council on Environmental Quality and Department of State, 1980).

Herman Kahn, who explained that the earth's most important resource is human ingenuity. Mankind has used technology and trade to overcome every scarcity in natural resources and there is no reason to believe that it should not continue to do so.[33]

In spite of this empirical and theoretical refutation, the environmental movement persists today. During the 1980s approximately 250 international environmental treaties and conventions were enacted. These initiatives have not fully consolidated the movement's power over environmental policymaking. But NGO familiarity with the elaborate framework of policymaking instruments now in place is helping the movement maintain and expand its influence. Environmental NGOs have learned important lessons from their successes and failures in the international arena. Not the least is that rhetoric and public relations are essential ingredients of public policy. Words matter.

'Sustainable Development': New Spin on an Old Argument

Environmentalists have become adept at altering their presentation to suit political and social changes, but they rarely change their arguments. In the 1970s they scared us with global cooling, which was supposedly caused by the sulphate aerosols emitted as a by-product of fossil fuel use. The answer: limit the use of fossil fuels. By the summer of 1988, it had become evident that the next ice age was a few thousand years off, so the environmentalists realigned themselves to promote global warming – an easier sell in the heat of July. Global warming was supposedly due to carbon dioxide, another by-product of the burning of fossil fuels, so the answer again was to limit the use of fossil fuels. How stupid or blind does one have to be to fail to see the irony in this? The objective of the environmentalists obviously has little to do with controlling the climate, which is as impossible as controlling the tides and everything to do with controlling use of energy and redistributing wealth.

The 1980s saw another change in the way in which environmentalists sold their arguments for limiting human endeavours. The intellectual opposition to the 'limits to growth' philosophy and the patent failure of the Club of Rome's predictions led to a shift towards an apparently more moderate ideology: 'sustainable development'. This idea was developed by the International Union for the Conservation of Nature (IUCN) as part of a 1980 consultation paper entitled *World Conservation Strategy: Living Resource Conservation for Sustainable Development,* which had been prepared for the United Nations Environment Programme (UNEP), WWF, the UN Food and Agriculture Organisation (FAO) and UNESCO.[34]

A year later, the concept received wider notice when a number of US environmental advocacy groups formed the Global Tomorrow Coalition, who stated

---

[33] Julian L. Simon and Herman Kahn, eds., *The Resourceful Earth* (Oxford: Basil Blackwell, 1984).
[34] *World Conservation Strategy: Living Resource Conservation for Sustainable Development,* (Gland: International Union for Conservation of Nature and Natural Resources, 1980).

that their goal was to work for 'a more sustainable, equitable global tomorrow'.[35] Sustainable development gave green activists an attractive new vocabulary, even though its political implications were little different from the limits-to-growth philosophy. Like the 1972 Club of Rome treatise, the 1980 IUCN *Strategy* propounds a theory of resource limitation: 'the planet's capacity to support people is being irreversibly reduced'. The *Strategy* blames an 'affluent minority' for consuming most of the world's resources. It demands heightened conservation awareness and more government regulation and it calls for population control measures to keep the alleged problem of resource consumption from worsening.

While sustainable development is not unlike limits-to-growth, it is noteworthy that nowhere does *World Conservation Strategy* explicitly call for a halt to economic growth.[36] The IUCN volume concedes the harshness of earlier environmentalist positions. 'Conservation is positive,' it asserts; it is 'for people'.[37] The *Strategy* also avoids blaming economic growth for environmental problems and it seldom predicts impending doom. Instead, sustainable development promises to solve problems by managing economic growth intelligently and democratically.

What is most distinctive about sustainable development is the way it combines the goals of environmentalism with those of economic development. Its supporters describe a political system in which conservation measures are integrated into all aspects of centralised government economic planning. Indeed, IUCN says a prosperous economy requires conservation controls: 'For development to be sustainable it must take into account social and ecological factors'.[38]

Sustainable development also requires large wealth transfers from industrial to developing nations. This merges the two forces that drove the UN agenda in the 1970s – the environmentalism of the Stockholm conference with the Third World's call for global wealth redistribution. The report warns: 'Humanity's relationship with the biosphere...will continue to deteriorate until a new international economic order is achieved'.[39]

The Brundtland Report

'Sustainable development' was just what the international environmental lobby needed. In 1982 UNEP held a conference to review its progress in the ten years since Stockholm. The delegates – a mix of government representatives, UN functionaries and IUCN participants – recommended the establishment of yet another elite body: a World Commission on Environment and Development. The following year the UN adopted Resolution 38/16 to create it and UN Secretary General Kurt Waldheim appointed its chairwoman, Dr Gro Harlem Brundtland,

---

[35] The Coalition included the Sierra Club, National Audubon Society, Environmental Defence Fund, Humane Society of the United States, Natural Resources Defence Council, Wilderness Society and Worldwatch Institute.
[36] *World Conservation Strategy,* Section 1.
[37] *World Conservation Strategy,* Section 1.4-1.5.
[38] Ibid.
[39] *World Conservation Strategy,* Section 1.2.

Prime Minister of Norway and head of the Norwegian Labour Party.[40]

For three years the commission held meetings which produced *Our Common Future*, a 350-page manifesto commonly known as the Brundtland Report.[41] With input from NGOs such as the WWF and IUCN,[42] the report sang the praises of 'sustainable development,' which it defined as:

> *Meeting the needs of the present without compromising the ability of future generations to meet their own needs. The concept of sustainable development does imply limits – not absolute limits but limitations imposed by the present state of technology and social organisation on environmental resources and by the ability of the biosphere to absorb the effects of human activities.*[43]

The Brundtland report is based on a model of 'market failure.' It argues that the market system is reaching its ecological limit: further reliance on markets to allocate resources will endanger the well-being of the world's populations. Instead, governments should make future management decisions about using the world's 'finite' resources by consulting a menu of policy options. These options range from environmental taxes to mandating an upper limit on consumption. Population growth also should be restricted by a series of increasingly coercive incentives.[44]

To achieve international 'equity,' the Commission proposed global taxes to transfer financial aid from the industrial West to less developed countries. Some of its suggested taxes are rather imaginative:

- taxes on revenues from the use of the 'international commons' (e.g. ocean fishing, seabed mining, transportation on the high seas and use of Antarctic resources) and from parking charges for geostationary communications satellites in space.
- taxes on international trade (e.g. a general trade tax; taxes on specific commodities, on 'invisible exports,' on balance of trade surpluses and on the consumption of luxury goods).[45]

The Commission asserted that 'sustainable global development requires that those who are more affluent adopt life-styles within the planet's ecological means – in their use of energy for example'.[46] This definition of 'development' essentially reverses its meaning.

The World Commission on Environment and Development was officially

---

[40] Matthias Finger, 'Environmental NGOs in the UNCED Process,' in Princen and Finger, *Environmental NGOs in World Politics*, 1994, p. 187.

[41] World Commission on Environment and Development, *Our Common Future*, (Oxford. Oxford University Press, 1987).

[42] Finger, p. 188.

[43] *Our Common Future*, p.8.

[44] *Our Common Future*; Porter and Brown, *Global Environmental Politics*, 1996, pp. 26-27.

[45] *Our Common Future*, pp. 341-2.

[46] *Our Common Future*, p.9.

dissolved after the Brundtland report was published in 1987. However, a year later its members then formed the Centre for Our Common Future.[47] With headquarters in Geneva, this organisation worked with key environmental groups[48] to promote the next landmark international conference – the UN Conference on Environment and Development (UNCED) – which was scheduled for 1992. The Centre also established alliances with 160 organisations in 70 countries to promote distribution and discussion of the Brundtland Report, which in effect became an international lobby. Their first opportunity to do what lobbies do – exert pressure by making their presence felt – was in Rio.

The Earth Summit in Rio de Janeiro (June 1992)

The UN Convention on Environment and Development (UNCED) was a very high profile conference. On June 1-12, 1992, dozens of world leaders and thousands of official and unofficial delegates and journalists gathered in Rio de Janeiro, Brazil. The Secretary General of UNCED was the ubiquitous Maurice Strong, who reprised his role in Stockholm of twenty years earlier. Known as the 'Earth Summit,' UNCED was the international version of Earth Day 1970 – an event to raise global awareness of environmental problems.

This massive undertaking broke new ground for NGOs. It was the largest gathering of such organisations at a UN-sponsored event – over 1400 officially accredited NGOs were present. More importantly, for the first time at a conference of this sort, the organisers officially involved NGOs in the lengthy, arduous and extremely important process of preparing the conference agenda.[49] Maurice Strong played a crucial role here in overcoming opposition from representatives of developing countries, who recognised that letting NGOs into the process threatened their own goals and interests.[50]

The UNCED process began in 1990 with a series of four Preparatory Committees – 'PrepComs' in UN-speak – that preceded the conference. At these meetings NGOs were able to work with officials in the UN bureaucracy and with delegations from UN member governments, drafting the negotiating text for consideration by the conference delegates. Some even served on government delegations.[51] Many governments also provided financial support so that activist groups could attend the meetings.[52]

At Rio itself, the NGOs sponsored a separate conference to parallel the official one. The 'Global Forum', which attracted 25 000 people from 167 countries, was intended to remind the official delegates that 1400 NGO official observers were watching their actions. Activists were on hand to stage protests, hold press

---

[47] Finger, p. 189.
[48] These included: the Sierra Club, National Wildlife Federation, NRDC, National Audubon Society, the Wilderness Society, the Nature Conservancy, WWF, IUCN and the World Resources Institute (Finger, p. 191).
[49] World Resources Institute, et al, *World Resources 1992-1993: A Guide to the Global Environment*, p. 219.
[50] Shabecoff, p.133.
[51] Porter and Brown, p.58.
[52] Shabecoff, p.149; Porter and Brown, p.58.

conferences and distribute press releases should their agenda be endangered.[53] More often, however, the participants tried to create the appearance of popular support for official Earth Summit initiatives. UN officials generally regarded them less as a threat than a validation of their work.[54]

At Rio the world's leaders signed several very important documents:

- *The Rio Declaration*: A broad statement of principles, which affirms 'sustainable development' as the foundation of international environmental policy.
- *Agenda 21*: A detailed 800-page blueprint, which outlines proposed government actions to implement sustainable development.
- *Framework Convention on Climate Change*: A treaty, signed by officials of 150 nations, the objective of which is to prevent global warming by curbing the emissions of carbon dioxide and other 'greenhouse gases.'
- *Convention on Biological Diversity*: A treaty, signed by officials of 98 nations, the objective of which is to protect the habitats of all living species, to manage ecosystems and to protect genetic resources by regulating scientific research and use of biotechnology.

Importantly, *Agenda 21* asserted that NGOs should play a permanent role in policymaking. All the NGOs present at Rio were invited to the follow-up activities. There was a number of important and immediate consequences of UNCED:

- The UN created a Commission on Sustainable Development and gave NGOs a prominent role in its deliberations.
- The World Bank created a Global Environment Facility (GEF), a $2 billion slush fund for Third World environment projects.
- The Clinton administration named James Gustave Speth to be head of the United Nations Development Programme (UNDP) and to refocus the Programme on sustainable development.[55]
- The UN scheduled conferences on topics such as Human Rights (Vienna, 1993), Small Island States (Barbados 1994), Population (Cairo, 1994), Social Development (Copenhagen, 1995), Women (Beijing, 1995) and Human Settlements (Istanbul, 1996).

---

[53] Of course, each group wanted to leave a lasting imprint on the proceedings. From vegetarianism and New Age philosophy to animal rights and women's rights, each NGO claimed the mantle of saving the planet. Youth groups organised demonstrations inside conference rooms to demand equal speaking time. Rock bands performed live concerts to support negotiations on biological diversity. Angry dissenters hung a large banner on Sugarloaf Mountain overlooking the city, denouncing the summit's slow progress. Throngs of people lined the beaches day and night to dance and chant for their favoured cause. The result was global cacophony. (Yolanda Kakabadse N., with Sarah Burns, 'Movers and Shapers: NGOs in International Affairs,' May 1994.)

[54] Peter M. Haas, Marc A. Levy and Edward A. Parson, 'Appraising the Earth Summit,' *Environment*, October 1992. See also Yolanda Kakabadse N., with Sarah Burns, 'Movers and Shapers: NGOs in International Affairs,' May 1994.

[55] Speth, then president of the World Resources Institute, had been chairman of President Carter's Council on Environmental Quality and he had helped write its *Global 2000* report.

53

- National and local governments around the world created bureaucracies to advise on how to implement *Agenda 21*.

Eco-imperialism: The Priorities of Global Governance

The governments of developing countries soon discovered that they did not share the policy priorities of developed governments and NGOs. It seemed to them that the rich countries of the North wanted to impose green rules on the poor countries of the South. It became clear to them that NGOs have a narrow view of environmental protection, which fails to account for the wide variation in circumstances that pertains across the globe. They suspected that the ideology of environmentalism was little more than 'eco-imperialism,' designed to protect the rich countries from the competitive advantages of poor countries. The sovereign states of Africa, Asia and Latin America resented this new form of colonialism.

The North-South rift was evident in the negotiations over a global forestry treaty. Developing countries, led by Malaysia, the Philippines and India rebuffed all US and European proposals to limit their use of tropical forests, calling the proposals a violation of their sovereignty. They said negotiations unfairly focused on restricting tropical forest harvest while excluding North American and European forests.

The call for global population control policies also generated fierce controversy. The Vatican, along with governments of Latin American and Islamic states lobbied successfully against *Agenda 21* policy recommendations calling for reductions in Third World population growth. They also forced debate on the morality of abortion and the sterilisation of women.

One Indonesian writer complained that 'an imperialistic attitude between First and Third World NGOs' led Northern environmental groups to be more concerned with their 'projects and campaigns than with the actual needs of Third World NGOs and communities'.[56] The ironic result was that UN conferences in the 1990s were strangely removed from the real concerns of the world's poor people. They focused on issues Northern NGOs wanted to discuss instead of on the interests of people in less developed countries, which, after all, are the majority of those represented by the UN.

While the environmental lobby has supported more Western aid to lessen world poverty, its promises cannot placate developing countries that fear being left behind in global competition. During the Earth Summit negotiations, the representatives of these countries tried with little success to underline the importance of their economic aspirations. Said one official from Ghana:

The development assistance which comes to us arrives with paternalistic and humiliating conditions...Basic development technology arrives with price tags that deepen not only our poverty but extends our condition of peonage to our so-called benefactors...It cannot be expected that, because of the present

---

[56] Hira Jhamtani, 'The Imperialism of Northern NGOs,' *Earth Island Jnl*, Summer 1992, p.5, cited in Shabecoff, p. 74.

perverse economic order, those who earn $200 per capita…are the ones to make sacrifices so that those who – by dint of the massive advantages of technology and an exploitative international economic regime – earn $10,000 per capita can breathe cleaner air or escape the tormenting discomforts that global warming may bring in its wake.[57]

The Green Attack on National Sovereignty

The sustainable development agenda is essentially an attack on national sovereignty. Sustainable development implicitly requires a comprehensive body of enforceable international law promulgated by multilateral institutions (such as the UN) and international treaty secretariats. Green advocates argue that this system of law will comprise a system of 'global governance.' Although global governance remains largely an idea, it can be and has been used to thwart private rights, local self-rule and the ordinary give-and-take of domestic national politics.

The concept of global governance was developed by the private Commission on Global Governance (CGG), a successor to the Brundtland Commission. The CGG is a group of twenty-eight world notables co-chaired by Ingvar Carlsson, former Prime Minister of Sweden and head of its Social Democratic Party and Shridath Ramphal, former Secretary-General of Guyana and former president of the World Conservation Union-IUCN. Maurice Strong is also a member of the Commission. It is funded by a variety of foundations and governments.[58]

In 1995 the CGG released *Our Global Neighbourhood,* a 410 page successor volume to the Brundtland report, *Our Common Future.*[59] Following two years of meetings, the Commission members outlined how the United Nations should undertake world economic planning. They proposed a vastly expanded role for an array of global political institutions. The CGG grandiosely proclaims that it will examine 'what the world community may set down as the limits of permissible behaviour in a range of areas and consider mechanisms…to encourage and if necessary enforce compliance with these norms'.[60] Environmental writer Ronald Bailey, writing in *National Review*, more simply calls CGG a 'creeping UN power grab'[61]

'Global governance is not global government,' writes the Commission, but it is hard to tell the difference. The Commission suggests that UN agencies should exercise authority that currently rests with national governments. It would add five

---

[57] Ibid.

[58] In 1993 the John D. and Catherine T. MacArthur Foundation of Chicago gave $500,000 to the CGG. It should be no surprise, then, that one of the American members is Adele Simmons, president of the MacArthur Foundation. The other US member is former World Bank president Barber Conable. Besides MacArthur, the Commission's other funders (amounts undisclosed) include the Ford and Carnegie foundations and the governments of the Netherlands, Norway, Sweden, Canada, Denmark, India, Indonesia, Switzerland, Japan and the European Commission. (*Our Global Neighbourhood,* p. 376 and Cliff Kincaid, 'Making Americans Pay: The MacArthur Foundation's Plan for a Global I.R.S.,' *Foundation Watch* (Capital Research Centre), September, 1996.)

[59] Commission on Global Governance, *Our Global Neighbourhood,* (New York: Oxford University Press, 1995) pp. 135-151.

[60] *Our Global Neighbourhood,* p. 369.

[61] Ronald Bailey, 'Who is Maurice Strong?' *National Review*, September 1, 1997.

new permanent members to the UN Security Council and eliminate the veto power currently held by the permanent Council members. NGOs, or what the Commission calls 'Civil Society Organisations,' would have a direct advisory role in the UN General Assembly.

The Commission recommends that the UN be funded by global taxes rather than depend on voluntary member-state contributions. One proposal, by Yale University economist James Tobin, would impose taxes on international currency transactions, which are 'of no intrinsic benefit in terms of economic efficiency'. Other tax ideas include special 'user fees' on airline tickets, ocean shipping, fishing, satellites and the electromagnetic spectrum. [62]

Commission supporters say too many world problems – climate change, ozone layer thinning, world trade – transcend national borders. Because national governments can no longer control the flow of capital, trade and telecommunications, they say a new source of political authority must be created. Jessica Tuchman Mathews, currently president of the Carnegie Endowment for International Peace, makes this point indirectly: 'The United Nations charter may still forbid outside interference in the domestic affairs of member states, but unequivocally 'domestic' concerns are becoming an endangered species'. [63] Less circumspect is Daniel C. Esty, a senior fellow at the Institute for International Economics. He says, 'In dealing with global environmental problems, it is only by surrendering a bit of national sovereignty and by participating in an international regime that we can ensure our freedom from environmental harms and protection of our own natural resources'. [64]

We are today some way from comprehensive global governance but there should be no doubt that supporters of the sustainable development agenda have it as their goal. Writing in 1992 as a vice president of the World Resources Institute, Mathews applauded the global warming treaty 'because it is so potentially invasive of domestic sovereignty'. She praised the climate treaty as a way of 'forcing governments to change domestic policies to a much greater degree than any other international treaty,' and hinted that it might jar Western governments as the Helsinki Accords had once destabilised the Eastern Bloc. [65] Mathews earlier likened the Rio Earth Summit to Allied preparations for a post-World War II economic system, 'in the same light we now see Bretton Woods, as one of the places where the rules of a new order were born'. [66]

Green groups praise sovereignty-robbing treaties because they have calculated that they stand to benefit. Organisations such as the World Resources Institute are already well-funded by large foundations (it was set up with a $15 million grant

---

[62] *Our Global Neighbourhood*, pp. 219-221.

[63] Mathews, 'Chantilly Crossroads,' *Washington Post*, February 10, 1991.

[64] Daniel C. Esty, *Greening the GATT: Trade, Environment and the Future*, Washington, DC, Institute for International Economics, July 1994, p. 93.

[65] Jessica Tuchman Mathews, speech to the Atlantic Forum, Federal News Service, May 18, 1992.

[66] Jessica Tuchman Mathews, 'Chantilly Crossroads.'

from the MacArthur Foundation in 1982); any action that empowers the United Nations is likely to empower them. Far from taking 'non-governmental' roles, they aspire to be extensions of a global governance system they have helped create.

When they imagine a world of global governance, NGOs are aiming for political control more than global environmental protection. But until their vision can be realised, they will continue to operate through the nation-state, urging it to share authority or act as a partner with international agencies and non-profits. Green visionaries Nazli Choucri and Robert C. North admit as much: 'We do not know how to manage and regulate the activities of individuals in the absence of institutional requisites of 'sovereign' states.'[67]

Elaine Dewar, a Canadian journalist who writes about the connections between environmental groups, government and big business, suspects that environmental issues have been used as a scare tactic:

How do you persuade [citizens in democracies] to give up sovereign national powers to govern themselves? How do you make them hand over power to supranational institutions they cannot affect, control, or remove? You make it seem as if this will serve their best interests. You terrify them with the grave dangers national governments cannot protect them from.[68]

Indeed, if all environmental threats are 'global,' then the environment may become for us what national security was during the Cold War. Jim MacNeill, Secretary-General of the (Brundtland) World Commission on Environment and Development echoes Dewar: 'The fears of nuclear conflict that once exercised enormous power over people's minds and translated into political support for today's massive defence establishments are declining. But certain environmental threats could come to have the same power over people's minds'.[69]

McNeill describes how a climate of fear over threats to the environment can be politically useful. But his thinking has moved well beyond that. McNeill was Strong's deputy at the Earth Summit and he understands that the political importance of UN environmental conferences is *the process* of organising them:

Part of what we are trying to achieve here is the process; we are trying to get countries to act internationally. The goals of sustainable development involve major compromises of sovereignty. There is no commitment yet to diluting national sovereignty. Before that happens we must have a credible system of international governance. But our job is not to do just what will happen in our lifetime. This process is an important step toward global governance, in which governments will have confidence and will surrender sovereignty.[70]

---

[67] Nazli Choucri and Robert C. North, 'Global Accord: Imperative for the Twenty-First Century,' in Nazli Choucri, *Global Accord*, (Cambridge, MIT Press, 1993), p.492.

[68] Elaine Dewar, *Cloak of Green*. (Toronto: James Lorimer & Co.) p. 251.

[69] Jim MacNeill, Pieter Winsemius, Taizo Yakushiji, *Beyond Interdependence: The Meshing of the World's Economy and the Earth's Ecology*, (New York: Oxford University Press, 1991) p. 69.

[70] Quoted in Shabecoff, p.157.

57

2. Global warming: The Politics of Pressure

During the first ten days of December 1997, international negotiators met in Kyoto, Japan to complete a global warming treaty. Officially, environmental groups and their allies in the UN were putting in place the capstone to a decade-long effort to prevent dangerous fluctuations in the earth's climate. But their real agenda was to control the world's use of energy and thereby to redistribute wealth. The end of the cold war and the fall of communism had discredited overt socialism, but here was a way to bring it in through the back door.

The environmental lobby's crusade against energy use began in the 1970s when the OPEC oil embargoes dominated the news. The Greens warned that the US would run out of fossil fuels – coal, oil and natural gas – unless the government discouraged Americans from using them. But political pressures for controls on energy subsided when the oil shortages of the 1970s became the gluts of the 1980s. Market forces gave firms an incentive to locate new fuel sources, cut prices and undercut activist demands for government intervention.

However, energy abundance did not deter the Green establishment for long. It found a new reason to restrict energy use: the spectre of changes in the earth's climate. In the 1970s environmentalists raised an alarm over 'global cooling,' a hypothesis derived from evidence that climate temperatures since about 1940 appeared to be in gradual decline. Some alarmists even predicted a coming Ice Age.[71] Environmentalists claimed that this situation as being exacerbated by the use of fossil fuels, which were causing a build-up of sulphate aerosols that were blocking out the sun. The policy prescription: burn less fossil fuel. But by the mid-1970s the cooling trend had petered out. The scare talk, however, did not. Environmentalists now turned their attention to refurbishing a climate theory of 'global warming.' By the late 1980s, all the major environmental organisations were espousing the theory and they demanded government action to restrict use of fossil fuel, its purported cause.

Organisations such as Greenpeace, Friends of the Earth and the Worldwatch Institute were in the forefront urging action to combat the 'greenhouse effect.' Their public relations campaign capitalised on the audacious predictions of some environmentalists inside government. NASA scientist Robert Watson had predicted in 1986 that the earth would warm by 1.8 degrees Fahrenheit by 1996.[72] The prediction proved false, but its assertion reinforced Green claims that a change in the weather meant changes to our way of life. 'We face the prospect of substantial economic loss and social disruption,' said Worldwatch Institute officials.[73]

Sensational predictions by academics also raised public fears that were used to thwart private sector energy use. Sherwood Rowland, professor of chemistry at the University of California at Irvine, warned: 'If you have the greenhouse effect going

---

[71] Douglas Colligan, 'Brace Yourself for Another Ice Age,' *Science Digest*, February 1973.

[72] John N. Maclean, 'Scientists Predict Catastrophes on Growing Global Heat Wave,' *Chicago Tribune*, June 11, 1986.

[73] Linda Werfelman, 'Study: Adjusting to Global Warming Will Cost Billions,' *United Press International*, July 19, 1986.

on indefinitely, then you have a temperature rise that will bring about the extinction of human life in 500 to 1,000 years'.[74] Such statements were exploited to great effect. The use of computer forecasts generated even more publicity. In 1987, the World Resources Institute programmed climate variables into a computer and devised a model that predicted global warming would raise sea levels by four feet.[75]

Hell on Earth

Environmentalists denounce modern civilisation as planet earth's greatest enemy. They scold us for driving, flying, manufacturing and consuming goods, growing food and for heating and cooling our homes. They do this in the name of limiting our use of fossil fuels, which they say cause climate change. These activities, it is true, cause gases to be emitted into the atmosphere, but what happens after that is unclear. There is, in fact, a natural greenhouse effect that does warm the atmosphere: it is what makes possible life on earth. Water vapour causes about 98 per cent of this warming. Carbon dioxide and other 'greenhouse gases' are responsible for a fraction of the remaining two per cent.

The environmental lobby claims that man's emissions of greenhouse gases will cause catastrophic global warming, resulting in the melting of the polar ice caps, rising seas, submerged islands and flooded coastal plains.[76] They say that the deserts will expand, reducing arable land and the productivity of agriculture; world food supplies will dwindle, causing widespread starvation; and there will be plagues of biblical magnitude.[77] Global warming, they claim, will prompt the spread of malaria, dengue fever and eastern equine encephalitis.[78]

The Eco-friendly Solution

To prevent this putative eco-catastrophe, the global warming lobby proposes drastic government policy changes. Worldwatch analyst Christopher Flavin says even the most modest proposals 'would mark a dramatic shift in direction and require wholesale changes in energy policy and land use planning around the world'.[79] But workers and consumers will be big losers if their homes, offices and factories,

---

[74] Stanley N. Wellborn 'The Skeptics Retreat: Earth's Temperature is Indeed Rising – and With it the Sea; Facing Life in a Greenhouse,' *US News & World Report*, September 29, 1986.

[75] Timothy Aeppel, 'Greenhouse Effect; Group Uses Computer Models to Forecast Global Climate,' *Christian Science Monitor*, April 13, 1987.

[76] The Natural Resources Defence Council (NRDC) predicts 'current rates of sea-level rise are expected to increase by 2 to 5 times due to both the thermal expansion of the oceans and the partial melting of mountain glaciers and polar ice caps.' (http://www.nrdc.org/bkgrd/gwcons.html) 'Sea level is projected to rise by six inches to as much as three feet' by the year 2100, predicts the EDF. (Dr. Janine Bloomfield and Sherry Showell, 'Global Warming: Our Nation's Capital at Risk,' Environmental Defence Fund, May 1997)

[77] . The Sierra Club warns that 'there are two main ways in which global warming will affect human health – extreme weather events (including heat waves) and infectious diseases.'(Comments by Dan Becker, Sierra Club, in 'The Great Global Warming Debate,' Pace Energy Project, Pace University School of Law, 'Global Warming Central' web site, http://www.law.pace.edu/env/energy/globalwarming.html.)

[78] The Environmental Defence Fund (EDF) describes in stark terms how encephalitis can strike horses and humans: 'Early symptoms include fever, headache, drowsiness and muscle pain, followed by disorientation, weakness, seizures and coma.' (Dr. Janine Bloomfield and Sherry Showell, 'Global Warming: Our Nation's Capital at Risk,' Environmental Defence Fund, May 1997, http://www.edf.org/pubs/Reports/WashingtonGW.)

[79] Christopher Flavin, *State of the World 1990* (New York: W. W. Norton & Co., 1990), p. 20.

appliances and vehicles are governed by the regulations that environmental groups demand. Frances Smith, executive director of Consumer Alert, warns that, 'consumers are direct users of oil, natural gas and electricity in their homes and for transportation. They are the end users of products – food, home building materials, appliances, furniture, cleaning and personal care products – whose manufacture and transport require energy'.[80] Living standards will decline if government regulations make energy more expensive and less abundant.

These concerns matter not to green groups, whose demands have grown increasingly strident. Greenpeace insists that the governments of industrial countries impose regulations to reduce carbon dioxide emissions twenty per cent below 1990 levels by the year 2005.[81] Other groups say this action, draconian as it may sound, will not avert impending catastrophe. 'To stabilise carbon dioxide concentrations in the atmosphere at their current levels,' writes Ozone Action, 'would require an immediate reduction of emissions by 50-70%, with further reductions later'.[82]

Reductions of this magnitude would require governments around the world to eliminate almost all carbon-based fuel use. What will replace the burning of coal, oil and natural gas, which comprise 90 per cent of the world's energy supply? Environmental lobby groups favour solar energy and they would phase out the automobile, replacing it with railways and other forms of mass transportation. Greenpeace exclaims, 'a future without fossil fuels is essential to preserve the environment from the serious risk of climate change'.[83] The drastic changes it proposes will cripple national economies, radicalise individual lifestyles and dramatically increase government regulation of producers and consumers. The more industrial – and prosperous – a country is, the harder it will be hit. According to MIT economist Richard Schmalensee, the global warming rules would be like experiencing the 'energy price hikes of the 1970s with a massive hangover'.[84]

Global Regulation for a Global Climate

Environmental lobbyists made their demands for a binding international treaty to regulate fossil fuel use in a highly deliberative and numbingly methodical way because they knew that if they were ever to obtain such a treaty, they would need to put in place a foundation of procedures and focused proposals.[85] First, they had to create a vague and open-ended framework treaty. In 1990, the UN established the aptly-named Intergovernmental Negotiating Committee for a Framework Convention on Climate Change (INC/FCCC). Administered by UNEP and the World Meteorological Organisation, the same groups that nurtured the ozone treaty

[80] Frances B. Smith, *The Global Warming Treaty: For US Consumers – All Pain, No Gain*, (Dallas: National Centre for Policy Analysis, Brief Analysis No. 238, August 20, 1997).

[81] 'The Climate Time Bomb,' Greenpeace International Climate Campaign, http://www.greenpeace.org/~climate/

[82] 'What would it take to stop climate change,' Ozone Action web site, www.essential.org/orgs/Ozone_Action/stopcc.html.

[83] Ibid.

[84] Richard Schmalensee, Massachusetts Institute of Technology, speech to American Council on Capital Formation Program on Climate Change Policy, Risk Prioritization and U. S. Economic Growth. Washington, DC, Sept. 11, 1996.

[85] Peter H. Sand, 'Innovations in International Environmental Governance,' *Environment*, November 1990, p. 19.

to fruition, the INC held a series of meetings to develop a treaty in time for the June 1992 Rio Earth Summit.

At Rio, the Framework Convention on Climate Change was signed by the representatives of more than 150 governments. but the real policymakers were the UN functionaries who worked on the draft text with environmental NGO activists over the course of two years of 'pre-negotiations.' The wording of the document is innocuous enough. All countries are exhorted to reduce their carbon dioxide emissions to 1990 levels by the year 2000. However, these restrictions are not binding; parties to the convention are obliged only to submit national reports to the convention secretariat. The Framework Convention lived up to its name, setting a timetable for subsequent regular meetings at which its interim commitments could be further interpreted and elaborated. Each meeting, called a 'Conference of the Parties' (COP), gives environmental lobbyists a chance to add something onto an earlier proposal and to build new expectations. At every meeting NGOs can either a) declare a small victory for the planet, or b) attack national governments for failing to save the planet. In any event, the framework convention process sets the stage for progressively manipulating soft treaty promises into more binding international obligations.

How the Climate Treaty Was Shaped

In March 1995, the first COP took place in Berlin with the primary objective of the organisers being to extend the requirements of the climate treaty, but lack of consensus and weak US support derailed these plans.[86] Instead of a strengthened treaty, the 1995 conference produced the 'Berlin Mandate,' a statement that merely declared the Rio convention inadequate and exhorted industrial countries to take action. Even worse, the developing countries took advantage of the listless proceedings to exempt themselves from future emissions targets. Any later binding protocol to the climate treaty would apply only to the industrial powers.

The issue of global warming could easily have lost all focus in Berlin were it not for the persistence of environmental groups. Roughly 1,000 NGOs attended the Berlin Summit and from the outset they lobbied hard to expand their rights of access to the proceedings.[87] Amongst other things they drafted the 'Green Paper.' This document, produced with the cooperation of sympathetic governments, adumbrated principles that formed the basis of the Berlin Mandate,[88] which in turn committed governments to meet in Kyoto, Japan, in December 1997 to negotiate targets and timetables to reduce carbon emissions.

While the conference was in session, the pressure groups also influenced the proceedings by publishing daily newsletters. *Eco*, produced by the Climate Action Network and *Earth Negotiations Bulletin*, from the Canada-based International

---

[86] The 1994 elections had brought a Republican majority to Congress, forcing the Clinton administration to pull back from the issue of global warming.
[87] *Earth Negotiations Bulletin*, Vol. 12, No. 12, (Winnipeg: International Institute for Sustainable Development, March 28, 1995).
[88] *Earth Negotiations Bulletin*, Vol. 12, No. 21, (April 10, 1995).

Institute for Sustainable Development (IISD), were diary-like journals that made editorial comments on the proceedings, targeted matters that activists cared about and proposed compromises for deadlocked issues.[89] Bombarding the negotiators with daily tips and admonitions, these and other newsletters provided the rhetoric and ideological tone that gave credence to radical ideas that delegates might not otherwise have considered. They also helped document the status of the issues being discussed and they reminded delegates that their positions were being monitored.

Despite their name, NGOs are not always 'non-governmental.' In fact, environmental pressure groups work hand in glove with governments that appreciate their work. This is apparent in the funding of the NGO newsletters. The Environment Ministries of Germany and the Netherlands contributed an undisclosed amount to the Climate Action Network to publish *Eco*. In her book *Cloak of Green*, Canadian journalist Elaine Dewar reveals that the publisher of *Earth Negotiations Bulletin* 'is almost entirely dependent on governments for its existence'. During the year-long period ending in March 1994, the IISD spent $530,000 to publish *Earth Negotiations Bulletin*. Over half that amount came out of the pockets of Canadian taxpayers.[90]

Clearly, international environmental groups do not represent grassroots citizens. They are well-connected and well-compensated advocates for increasing the regulatory powers of government bureaucracies. Global warming lobbyists shower delegates with constant written and personal attention and this usually has its intended effect in international treaty negotiations. Delegates begin to think that radical proposals have strong public support. *Eco* explains, 'NGOs contribute to the success of these regimes at every level by developing the science, informing the public, marshalling political support, prodding recalcitrant negotiators and providing front line troops to implement and monitor these regimes'.[91]

Kyoto Countdown

To prepare for Kyoto, NGOs cemented their relationships with national and international environmental agencies. Of particular importance was the UN Intergovernmental Panel on Climate Change (IPCC), which was funded and controlled by environmental agencies and they were not afraid to use their power. In early 1996, the IPCC published a report on the science of climate change. When the scientists who were the actual authors of the report failed to link variations in climate temperature to human activity, the lead author, who favoured the view that man was causing global warming, simply re-wrote the parts with which he disagreed. Frederick Seitz, the former president of the National Academy of Sciences, called the incident the most 'disturbing corruption of the peer review

---

[89] *Eco* has been funded by the Environment Ministries of Germany and the Netherlands.

[90] All told, the IISD received $23 million in taxpayer dollars over a five year period; in some years it had no other source of revenue. Moreover, it did not hurt IISD that its board of directors included Maurice Strong. (Elaine Dewar, *Cloak of Green: Business, Government and the Environmental Movement*, (Toronto: James Lorimer & Co., 1995) pp. 387-394.)

[91] *Eco* NGO Newsletter, Bonn, Climate Action Network, March 4, 1997.

process' he had ever witnessed. He warned that the effect of the re-write was 'to deceive policy makers and the public into believing that the scientific evidence shows human activities are causing global warming'.[92]

The re-written report approved a politically distorted interpretation of science that benefited the UN's global regulatory aspirations and that could be used to steer the Kyoto climate treaty negotiations. It asserted that human activities have a 'discernible' influence on climate. The environmental pressure groups used the lead author's editorial revision to distort the report's meaning. They announced that science had 'proved' the need for drastic energy policy changes and they smeared as dishonest industry propagandists any climate scientist who disagreed with an official UN finding. Environmental NGOs immediately picked up on the implications of this: 'The IPCC report serves a clear warning: Humans have begun to influence earth's climate and the outcome could be disastrous for many people and natural places,' said Michael Oppenheimer of the Environmental Defence Fund (EDF).[93]

Patience and determination was paying off for the global warming lobby. In 1996 the planets of international policy and domestic US politics came into alignment. As the UN report was being drafted, the Clinton administration was searching for issues that could be advanced without congressional interference and that would help mobilise the Democratic Party's base of environmental supporters. Global warming lobbyists were energised by the knowledge that the Administration would go to Kyoto if it was re-elected. A tightly coordinated coalition of activists began preparing a multi-million dollar two-year lobbying campaign on global warming.

Under the aegis of the Climate Action Network, pressure groups such as EDF, Natural Resources Defence Council, Sierra Club and Environmental Information Centre sprang into action. They scheduled a series of 'town meetings' in Austin, Boston, Miami, San Diego, San Francisco and Seattle.[94] The meetings featured Clinton administration scientists and environmental officials and their purpose was to generate scare stories in the media about how global warming would devastate local economies and the lifestyles of area residents. This gave rise to many absurd and frightening stories about how global warming would destroy local tourism, fishing, skiing, real estate and forestry.[95]

As the public campaign for Kyoto was underway, environmental groups privately offered the Administration their advice. On September 15, 1997, President Clinton, Vice President Gore and Interior Secretary Bruce Babbitt met with leaders of fourteen environmental lobby groups to finalise plans for a pre-

[92] Frederick Seitz, 'A Major Deception on 'Global Warming,'' *Wall Street Journal*, June 12, 1996.

[93] 'EDF Lauds IPCC Report,' Environmental Defence Fund news release, December 15, 1995.

[94] Peter H. Stone, 'The Heat's On,' *National Journal*, July 26, 1997.

[95] 'Climate Change Town Meeting in CA Ponders Local Risks,' *Greenwire*, October 15, 1996.

Kyoto White House conference on global warming.[96] Clinton and Gore would sell the treaty to the press. The environmental lobbyists advised them to take a hard anti-industry line.

Carnival in Kyoto (December 1997)

From 1 to 10 December 1997 an estimated 10,000 people gathered in Kyoto, Japan, in order to witness or participate in the international negotiations that would lead to the signing of a treaty to limit the emission of greenhouse gases. While the world's governments sent delegates to negotiate a serious agreement, the world's non-governmental organisations assembled to stir the pot of activism. Over 3,500 people attended the Kyoto conference as NGO lobbyists, more than double the 1,500 official delegates. About twenty American environmental organisations were represented and each had pockets deep enough to pay for several participants. But the American activists were easily outnumbered by Greens from Europe and Asia. A Japanese NGO confederation, the Kiko Forum, alone deployed 385 participants.

The global environmental lobby was determined to demonstrate in the most graphic ways possible the significance of the climate change treaty. For instance, activists demanded that conference organisers impose 'climate discipline' on the negotiations. This led to the distribution of a notice informing delegates that they would have to tolerate a cooler indoor climate in order to reduce greenhouse gas emissions. Said one flyer, 'it will be required that we accept a new lifestyle, including wearing warmer clothes, which enables us to live comfortably in spite of lower temperature in winter'.

NGOs convinced the Kyoto International Conference Hall to set the temperature of heating equipment 'at no higher than 20 degrees Centigrade [68 degrees F]'.[97] However, they failed to take into account the conference hall's inadequate insulation, which lowered temperatures in many parts of the building and forced the ten thousand shivering conference-goers to don coats and scarves. Conference staff distributed 100 shawls to women delegates; they featured the words 'Smart Life with Energy Saving.'

Outside, the Korean Federation of Environmental Movements arranged attention-getting props. Its members covered trees and shrubbery with signs reading, 'Cool the Earth, Save Us,' 'Please: Gas Masks!' 'No Nukes, No Fossil Fuels for Us,' 'Silent but Angry,' and 'Reduce GHGs [greenhouse gases] 20%'.[98] It did not seem to have occurred to the demonstrators that the growth of their economy – one of the most remarkable success stories of the latter part of the twentieth century – could not have occurred without increased use of fossil fuels; that they owed their wealth and possibly even their lives to this economic growth; and that to reduce consumption of fossil fuels would certainly slow this growth and possibly reverse it

---

[96] 'Clinton Meets with Environmentalists in Advance of White House Conference,' Bureau of National Affairs, *BNA Daily Environmental Report*, September 16, 1997.

[97] Flyer from the Energy Conservation Centre, Japan, distributed to all Kyoto conference participants.

[98] S. Fred Singer, 'The Week That Was,' December 7-13, 1997, http://www.sepp.org/weekwas/dec7_13.html.

– throwing millions of Koreans back into the poverty whence they had come.

In front of the entrance to the conference hall activists placed three ice statues carved in the shape of penguins. The statues were supposed to melt during the day, dramatising before television cameras the 'warming' of the earth's climate. However, Mother Nature would not cooperate and the sculptures remained standing. When a warmer day did arrive, activists held a prayer meeting around the melting penguins and prayed for forgiveness. (Greenpeace's solar-powered coffee maker was just as luckless. Rainy and overcast days thwarted the alternative fuels solar cell panel in the Greenpeace $20,000 'kitchen of tomorrow' display. Those seeking free solar-brewed coffee were turned away when the sun failed to shine for three days.[99])

A massive Tyrannosaurus Rex constructed of scrap metal stood at the back door to the conference hall – a symbol of the obsolescent wastefulness of modern society. Yet the conference itself generated three tons of waste paper in its first four days.[100] NGOs covered every table in the conference hall with so many fliers and pamphlets that journalists in the press centre complained.

Some green antics were foolish but funny, while others revealed the fanatic's self-righteousness. Most NGO representatives from North America and Europe travelled to Kyoto by plane, while some believed the claim that one plane passenger caused as much global warming as eight persons travelling by train. This led three dozen purists to travel for three weeks on board the 'Climate Train' from western Europe across Siberia, then by ferry over the Sea of Japan and on to Kyoto on bicycle.[101] 'We felt it important to travel to this conference in a way that has as little impact on the climate as possible,' said Richard Scrace, a director of Great Britain's Green Party. Climate Train passengers criticised their Japanese hosts for not establishing bicycle lanes to make their pedalling easier.[102]

While silliness is perhaps inevitable in all large public gatherings, civility was also a casualty of the global warming policy debate. Activists wearing masks of prominent politicians ridiculed the world's leaders; someone defaced a Nuclear Energy Institute display; and about thirty activists stormed an Esso gas station in downtown Kyoto. While chanting protests against Exxon, Esso's corporate parent, they stopped station employees from approaching gas pumps and raised a banner denouncing gasoline.[103] Jeremy Leggett, a Greenpeace activist and solar power advocate, characterised opposition to the climate treaty as 'a new form of crime against humanity'.[104] A Leggett seminar open to 'accredited press and invited NGOs only' was entitled 'History of the Fossil Fuel Disinformation Campaign at

[99] S. Fred Singer, 'The Week That Was,' December 7-13, 1997, http://www.sepp.org/weekwas/dec7_13.html.

[100] Kahori Sakane, 'Kyoto Climate Conference Disposes of Tons of Paper,' *Daily Yomiuri*, December 6, 1997.

[101] Joseph Coleman, 'Global Climate Meeting Attracts Passionate and Powerful With Global Warming,' *Associated Press*, December 4, 1997.

[102] Akiko Shiozaki, 'Group Makes 3-Week Journey to Bring Message,' *Asahi News Service*, December 2, 1997.

[103] 'Thirty Conference Participants Stage Protest at Esso Filling Station in Kyoto,' *Kyoto News Service*, December 4, 1997; Willis Witter, 'Activists Demonstrate at Kyoto Conference,' *Washington Times*, December 6, 1997.

[104] Leyla Boulton, 'Japan Attacked as Climate Deal Nears,' *Financial Times*, December 5, 1997.

the Climate Talks.'

UN officials and representatives of the American government abetted the activists' sense of self-importance. Members of the US delegation, many of them former environmental activists, had close working relationships with the Greens.[105] Every day, the US delegation briefed NGOs on the state of the negotiations, but they made a point of hosting separate ninety-minute meetings for environmental NGOs and industry NGOs. There were many more environmental NGOs than industry groups.

When US Vice President Al Gore arrived in Kyoto on December 8, the eighth day of the conference, he left no doubt where he stood. In a five-minute presentation to a small, hand-picked group of US delegates and reporters, Gore publicly instructed American negotiators 'to show increased negotiating flexibility' on the treaty, 'one with realistic targets and timetables, market mechanisms and the meaningful participation of key developing countries'.[106] 'The most vulnerable part of the Earth's environment is the very thin layer of air clinging near the surface of the planet,' Gore intoned. 'We are altering the relationship between the Earth and the Sun'. Changing mankind's behaviour would require 'humility because the spiritual roots of our crisis are pride'. Gore urged his NGO compatriots to be patient. 'This is the step-by-step approach we took in Montreal ten years ago to address the problem of ozone depletion. And it is working'.

S. Fred Singer, an atmospheric physicist and founder of the Science and Environmental Policy Project, described the spectacle of press coverage surrounding Gore's long-awaited '16,000 miles for five minutes' address. Only fifty hand-picked reporters were allowed inside the conference hall, while the rest were dispatched to watch the Vice President on large screen televisions:

> As Gore's giant image appeared on screen, hordes of reporters crowded around each video projector, taking photographs of the TV, pressing their microphones up to the speakers and straining to catch every word emanating from this New Age Big Brother.[107]

At a news conference immediately after Gore's remarks, the environmental NGOs attempted to characterise for reporters the meaning of his cryptic, emotional speech. But their 'spin' was mixed. Some lashed Gore with the catcalls normally reserved for political enemies, while other welcomed him as a passionate partisan for the planet.

European Greens were unanimous in denouncing Gore as a traitor and lackey of Big Oil. Greenpeace International said 'the speech was strong on rhetoric but basically full of hot air'.[108] WWF attacked Gore as 'unwilling to commit to a

---

[105] One member of the US delegation, the State Department's Rodrigo Prudencio, was a former activist employed by the National Wildlife Federation.

[106] Bonner R. Cohen, 'Gore: US Must Show Increased Flexibility in Kyoto,' *Earth Times*, December 9, 1997.

[107] S. Fred Singer, 'The Week That Was,' December 7-13, 1997, http://www.sepp.org/weekwas/dec7_13.html.

[108] Shoichi Nasu, 'Critics Divided on Gore Speech,' *Daily Yomuiri*, December 9, 1997.

meaningful target for reductions in line with the other industrialised nations'.[109] Friends of the Earth International reverently read aloud excerpts of Gore's 1992 book, *Earth in the Balance* and challenged the vice president to re-read the book himself.[110] The group distributed leaflets that depicted Clinton and Gore as wooden dummies sitting on the lap of a wealthy Texas oil man in a cowboy hat. 'The White House must now make a choice between protecting people from climate disaster or letting a few big companies make massive profits at our – and our children's – expense'.[111]

US-based NGOs were more loyal to their champion. The National Environmental Trust gently nudged Gore, reminding him of his own 1992 remarks criticising President Bush's trip to the Rio Earth Summit. '[This issue] is about far more than hopping on a plane for a quick photo opportunity ... and then flying back with a meaningless treaty that has no commitments in it'. The Union of Concerned Scientists praised Gore for demonstrating the 'significant leadership we are looking for'.[112] Fred Krupp, director of the Environmental Defence Fund, commented that Gore 'has significantly raised the environmental expectations of the conference and provided the key to unlocking the global gridlock which has paralysed the negotiating process'.[113]

The Politics of Green Imperialism

Environmental activists were united in their demand that the world's most advanced economies undertake major reductions in the emission of greenhouse gases. The most drastic demand came from a Korean activist group, which carried a sign with the threat: 'Delegates, we will make you Rowing Boats Slaves in the Water World if you fail to stop global warming'. The Sierra Club called for a 20 per cent cut in emissions from 1990 levels beginning no later than 2005. Other organisations liked the idea of starting with the European Union proposal of a 15 per cent reduction by 2010 – and ending with zero emissions.

But here's the rub. If the United States, the European Union and Japan restricted their economies' use of energy, then competitors from less-developed countries would have an advantage in international markets. American labour unions, in particular, feared US industries would have every incentive to relocate their operations to Third World countries not covered by the treaty's mandates.

Clinton, ever-sensitive to such domestic political considerations, also found himself bound by the reality that the Republican-led Senate would have the final say over whether to ratify any agreement struck at Kyoto. In July 1997, the Senate voted on the Byrd-Hagel resolution, which specified that any climate protocol should not damage the US economy and should not exempt developing countries from emission reduction requirements. The resolution passed by 95-0. The Clinton

---

[109] 'Gore: US Must Show Increased Flexibility in Kyoto,' *Earth Times*, December 9, 1997.
[110] 'Friends of the Earth Calls on Gore: Read Your Book Al!' press release, December 8, 1997.
[111] Friends of the Earth, 'Greenhouse Effect, Whitehouse Defect.'
[112] 'Critics Divided on Gore Speech,' *Daily Yomuiri*, December 9, 1997.
[113] 'Gore: US Must Show Increased Flexibility in Kyoto' *Earth Times*, December 9, 1997.

administration reacted by asking Third World countries to accept binding emissions reductions on their own economies. It pledged to secure the 'meaningful participation' of major Third World economies in emissions reduction.

This, however, would be no easy task. Led by China and India, Third World countries adamantly opposed actions that would slow their economic progress to solve what they perceived as the West's environmental problems. Currency devaluation, capital flight and economic collapse were threatening Thailand, Indonesia and South Korea. Other countries could succumb to the 'Asian flu' unless the region's economic problems were addressed.

The Chinese government's position was particularly strong. It rejected any limits on its own emissions and it opposed any reference in the treaty to voluntary restrictions.[114] All other developing countries supported the Chinese. Third World negotiators even deleted a proposed treaty provision that would have allowed developing countries to undertake emissions cuts at a later date.

Although the Kyoto talks were classified as a negotiation on the environment, delegates were actually hammering out an accord over energy, the life-blood of a global economy. Whether people can heat or cool their homes, cook meals and drive vehicles to productive jobs depends on the availability and cost of energy. This was well-understood by UN officials, who affirmed, 'The key is to put into place effective national policies to influence the behaviour of the industry and consumers.'[115]

After eleven days of private negotiations, the conference settled on a final treaty. It looked very different from what the Clinton administration had first proposed. The original Administration proposal would have cut carbon emissions to 1990 levels by 2010, a 34 per cent reduction from what they otherwise would be in that year. But this position was contingent on getting Third World countries to agree to cut their emissions too. The treaty that was agreed to by 167 countries contained these major provisions:[116]

- Six 'greenhouse gases' were targeted for emissions reduction.
- The US, Japan, the EU and other industrialised countries agreed to cut aggregate emissions of greenhouse gases by 5 per cent below 1990 levels by 2012.
- Developing Countries would not cut emissions at all.
- A framework would be established to permit the US, Canada, Japan, Russia, Australia and New Zealand to trade emissions credits. This 'umbrella' concept allows countries to buy and sell credits from each other in order to reduce the overall cost of meeting the emission reduction targets.
- A 'Clean Development Mechanism' would be created, which would allow

---

[114] Thomas Gale Moore, 'The Yellow Brick Road from Kyoto,' *World Climate Report*, Vol. 3 No. 10, February 2, 1998.

[115] Ramesh Jaura, 'Global Warming: NGOs Concerned About Fate of Kyoto Treaty,' *Inter Press Service*, December 11, 1997.

[116] Bonner R. Cohen, 'Battle over Kyoto Protocol Already Under Way,' *Earth Times*, December 13, 1997.

industrial countries to earn emission reduction credits when they gave energy efficient technologies to Third World countries.

The US Senate's reaction to this was unambiguous. The Kyoto Protocol did not meet the requirements of the Byrd-Hagel resolution, so Senators Chuck Hagel and Trent Lott, the Majority Leader, declared it 'dead on arrival.'[117] The Clinton Administration conceded that the treaty had failed to garner the meaningful participation of developing countries and it elected to withhold the treaty from Senate consideration until at least late 1998. However, the failure to secure developing country agreement at the Fourth COP in Buenos Aires has led to this being put off once more.

The NGO Strategy: Good Cop, Bad Cop

In order to understand the influence of NGOs on the outcome of Kyoto and its aftermath, it is helpful to understand how the different NGOs positioned themselves. Although many NGOs share broadly similar goals (limiting energy use in developed countries and redistributing resources to the developing world), their differences often added strength to their arguments. Each NGO acted out a different role, some praising government for their bold actions, others criticising them for the same actions. This good-cop bad-cop routine worked well at Kyoto and was continued afterwards.

The WWF had proposed that industrial countries cut their emissions by at least five per cent below 1990 levels by 2007.[118] The Kyoto Protocol comes remarkably close in calling for a five per cent cut by 2012. Nevertheless, a WWF statement issued immediately after the agreement was finally reached read: 'The treaty will fail to properly reduce the threat of climate change because key players – in particular the US and Japan – have refused to set realistic targets for emission reductions'.[119]

Greenpeace attacked the Kyoto Protocol as 'a tragedy and a farce' with too many 'loopholes'. 'This deal provides absolutely no protection from the increasing environmental and economic damage that the burning of coal and oil will continue to unleash on the world'. Friends of the Earth said that a five per cent emissions reduction is 'far below the 15 per cent reduction proposed by the European Union'.[120]

Some organisations played an intermediate role; the Sierra Club's Daniel F. Becker managed to say two things at once. He applauded the treaty as cause for celebration because it helped alter lifestyles in the industrialised world. But he also observed that the Kyoto Protocol was 'too weak and the loopholes too large, to protect our families'.[121]

---

[117] Statement by US Senator Chuck Hagel, press release, December 10, 1997.

[118] Shoichi Nasu, 'NGOs Blast Latest Gas Cut Proposal,' *Daily Yomuiri*, December 9, 1997.

[119] 'Non-governmental Organisations Not Satisfied with Protocol,' Kyodo News Service, Tokyo, December 11, 1997.

[120] 'NGOs Criticise Kyoto Agreement,' *Daily Yomuiri*, December 12, 1997.

[121] Jaura, 'Global Warming: NGOs Concerned About Fate of Kyoto Treaty.'

Perhaps the most vocal of the 'good cops' was the National Environmental Trust (NET), whose president Philip Clapp proclaimed, 'This is more than the environmental community has done on any single issue in 10 years'.[122] NET executive vice president Tom Wathen crowed, 'We believe the environmental community scored a monumental victory'.[123]

NET seems to have been instrumental in engineering US media support for Kyoto. NET executive vice president Tom Wathen prepared a particularly revealing memorandum on 11 December 1997, 'Climate Change Victories at Kyoto', for distribution to the organisation's supporters, which explains the communications strategy NET used to push the global warming agenda into the mass media. The memo notes that NET coordinated daily conference calls with as many as fifty reporters from national media outlets. It placed opinion-editorials on global warming for Enron Corporation chairman Kenneth Lay in the *Houston Chronicle, Austin American Statesman, Salt Lake Tribune* and *Omaha World Herald* and for former British Environment Minister John Gummer in the *Washington Post, Denver Post, Tampa Tribune, Pittsburgh Post-Gazette and Milwaukee Journal Sentinel*.[124] NET conducted eight 'town meetings' around the US, which generated much television, radio and print coverage. Wathen also claims NET mailings and briefings with editorial boards generated over 100 favourable editorials in major newspapers across the country. He says they helped change the tone of media stories which 'no longer presented global warming as just a theory over which reasonable scientists could differ'.

Concerned that television news producers were forced to rely on stock footage of parched fields to show the effect of global warming, NET designed special computer animations that television news programmes could use. They depicted how global warming would cause the flooding of fifteen American cities! ABC, NBC, CBS and CNN used this animation and it also was routed to local stations via satellite.

NET also took credit for temporarily suspending its opponents' television advertising campaign on the Cable News Network (CNN). On 2 October 1997 CNN announced that it would not show television commercials prepared by the Global Climate Information Project (GCIP) that criticised the Clinton administration position on the proposed treaty. GCIP is a coalition of car makers, farmers, steel mills, petroleum refiners, electricity producers and coal mining unions. It argued that treaty proposals unfairly hurt the American economy by raising US energy costs while exempting developing countries from compliance. The industry group's pithy slogan was: 'It's not global and it won't work.'

CNN is a division of media conglomerate Time-Warner, Inc. and the creation

---

[122] 'Intense Lobbying Against Global Warming Treaty,' *New York Times*, December 7, 1997.

[123] However, many environmentalists think NET is a front organisation preparing for the Gore for President campaign in 2000. Indeed, Philip Clapp was a top aide to former Senator Tim Wirth and his political resume includes Environmentalists for Clinton-Gore. (Mark Boal, 'Gore's Greens,' *Village Voice*, January 20, 1998.)

[124] Memorandum of Tom Wathen, executive vice president, National Environmental Trust, 'Climate Change Victories at Kyoto,' Washington, DC, December 11, 1997.

of Ted Turner, a major donor to environmental groups. CNN explained that the Environmental Information Centre (NET's name at the time) had demonstrated to its satisfaction that the commercials were inaccurate and misleading.[125] This decision provoked an outcry from treaty opponents who suspected Turner's involvement. Senator Chuck Hagel called for a congressional inquiry,[126] and, in a full-page *Wall Street Journal* ad, GCIP warned Time Warner chairman and CEO Gerald Levin against actions that would make it 'a party to censorship.'[127] Indeed, the decision coincided with Turner's announcement that he would donate $1 billion to the United Nations. (CNN eventually reversed its decision, but the disruption upset the strategy of those opposed to an international climate control treaty.)

Of course, one can be somewhat sceptical of a memo that congratulates itself on the genius of its own communications strategy. But the NET memo reveals the energy and cleverness that goes into good public relations. And the memo reveals something more. It makes clear that environmental pressure groups have developed an effective dual strategy of reward and punishment.

NET takes credit for orchestrating a lobbying campaign that it says enabled President Clinton to select 'the most ambitious proposal' from a range of options. NET's Wathen claims that the President did so, 'in part because of the substantial amount of national and local media, grassroots activity and polling information on climate change generated by NET and its campaign partners'.

At the same time Wathen describes how NET delivered a letter to the White House 'expressing outrage with the weakness of the Clinton-Gore proposal'. A NET 'rapid response team' funnelled inside information on the climate talks from Kyoto back to environmental activists in the US, who then sent hundreds of letters to the Vice President making specific demands. Ultimately, NET credits this strategy with breaking a deadlock by getting Gore to intervene and instruct the State Department to toughen its negotiating position. Initially calling for cutting emissions to 1990 levels by 2010, the Administration agreed to a seven per cent reduction below 1990 levels by 2012.

The result of these mixed responses from the environmental community is that politicians are made to feel somewhat pleased with themselves for having achieved anything at all, whilst being acutely aware that they will face continued pressure to agree to more and more onerous restrictions in the future.

---

[125] David Bauder, 'CNN Pulls Ads on Global Warming,' *Associated Press*, October 2, 1997.

[126] Ken Foskett, 'Treaty Opponents Object as CNN Pulls Global Warming Ads,' *Atlanta Journal*, October 4, 1997.

[127] Phil Kloer, 'CNN Changes Tune, Will Air Banned Ads,' *Atlanta Journal and Constitution*, October 10, 1997, p. 4H; David Bauder, 'CNN Reverses Stance on Disputed Ads,' *Associated Press*, October 9, 1997.

3. Trade and Environmentalism

Environmental pressure groups that promote the idea of protecting the environment by regulating trade have made themselves major players in policy and political battles over international trade agreements.[128] The environmental lobby has seized the initiative by arguing that the 'global environment' is affected by trade and by demanding a role in trade negotiations. Green groups have lobbied tenaciously for limits on the North American Free Trade Agreement (NAFTA) and the World Trade Organisation, demonstrating that even in inhospitable territory they can influence policy and the wealth of nations.

Environmental organisations are joined in this battle by other lobbyists whose concerns are often more explicitly protectionist. For example, labour organisations are primarily concerned to keep jobs in the particular sectors they represent. The consequence is inevitably a reduction in the efficiency of resource allocation and a reduction in the international competitiveness of the firms that are 'protected'. The long-term consequences of such protection is often devastating for the industries that are protected, because foreign companies become so much more efficient that they are able to out-compete the protected firms in every market but that which is protected. This is precisely what happened to America's car manufacturers in the 1970s and 1980s – and it has taken twenty years for them to regain their competitiveness.

Tuna and Trade

In 1991 a GATT tribunal highlighted the trade and environment issue by ruling against a US trade embargo of Mexican tuna imports. Environmental groups earlier had filed suit to force the Bush administration to move against Mexico for failing to protect dolphins entrapped by the tuna nets of Mexican fishing vessels.[129] Citing the 1972 Marine Mammal Protection Act, the Earth Island Institute claimed that US trade sanctions should be imposed against Mexico for failing to enact dolphin protection measures. The GATT tribunal, however, found that a US embargo on Mexican tuna violated GATT rules, which prohibited enforcement of a nation's environmental regulations outside its own jurisdiction.

The 'tuna-dolphin case' infuriated environmental groups and they spent $50,000 on full-page ads in major newspapers across the country to assail the GATT. Environmental, labour and liberal farm organisations opposed to free trade coalesced under the Citizens Trade Campaign, which spent $400,000. The coalition included Ralph Nader's Public Citizen (a 'consumer' watchdog), Friends of the Earth, Greenpeace, National Farmers Union, National Family Farm Coalition, the International Union of Electricians, the Amalgamated Clothing and Textile Workers Union and the International Ladies Garment Workers Union. Public Citizen plastered Washington, DC sidewalks with posters of 'GATTzilla,' a

---

[128] Robert Costanza, John Audley, Richard Borden, Paul Elkins, Carl Folke, Silvio O. Funtowicz and Jonathan Harris, 'Sustainable Trade: A New Paradigm for World Welfare,' *Environment*, June 1995.
[129] Porter and Brown, *Global Environmental Politics*, p. 131.

Godzilla-like monster with the earth in its jaws, crushing a dolphin in one hand, pouring out a barrel of DDT with the other and kicking over the US Capitol building. 'GATT is Coming,' the signs warned, 'What You Don't Know Will Hurt You'.

Environmental groups lobbied delegates to put restrictions on the GATT at the 1992 Earth Summit in Rio. Green groups, however, discovered that developing countries at the Rio conference were distrustful of their ideas. India and South Korea, in particular, worried that developed countries would cite environmental failings to justify protectionist trade barriers against their exports.

NAFTA: Environment, Trade and Protection

The trade-environment nexus became firmly established during the 1992-93 debate over ratification of the North American Free Trade Agreement (NAFTA). The United States, Canada and Mexico had agreed to form a trade bloc like the European Community. Green groups wanted to change the treaty and they did their homework. After the 1992 election, they lobbied the new Clinton administration to add environmental restraints to the NAFTA agreement that the Bush administration had already negotiated.

The Kyoto strategy of good cop-bad cop was prefigured during the NAFTA negotiations. Some groups, such as the National Wildlife Federation and Environmental Defence Fund, said that they had no fundamental objections to trade. They were prepared to accept NAFTA now and pursue environmental restrictions later, while some groups, such as Public Citizen and the Sierra Club, said they would have been happy to see NAFTA defeated. They threatened to work with labour unions to defeat the agreement unless heavy environmental restrictions were added. The bad cops pressed Congress to reject NAFTA, while the good cops used the threat of opposition as leverage to obtain a seat at the NAFTA negotiating table.

During congressional testimony, US trade representative Mickey Kantor revealed that the purpose of NAFTA harmonisation was more than environmental protection: it was trade protection.[130] Trade regulations could restrict market access to foreign products under the guise of environmental, health and worker safety concerns. For Kantor, the environmental side agreements were a way to prevent certain kinds of import competition from Mexico:

I think the question for us in looking at the NAFTA and these supplemental agreements is this: can we harmonise standards upwards to lessen Mexico's trade advantages as well as to help the environment and worker standards...in order to ensure that we don't adversely affect US workers and US visitors to the extent they're being affected now.

In August 1993, Mexico, Canada and the US agreed to an environmental

---

[130] US Trade Representative Mickey Kantor, 'Side Agreements to the North American Free Trade Agreement,' Senate Environment and Public Works Committee hearing, Reuters Transcript Report, March 16, 1993.

accord that was incorporated into NAFTA. A report from the US Trade Representative indicated that the Administration had followed many of the environmental lobby's recommendations.[131] The treaty established a Commission on Environmental Cooperation that was authorised to implement NAFTA provisions on the environment, monitor compliance and promote harmonisation of environment regulations among the NAFTA parties. It also created a separate North American Development Bank (NADBANK), NAFTA's version of the World Bank, to finance roughly $8 billion in public works projects and environmental spending in the border region, an area the environmentalists said was particularly degraded by trade.

At a September 1993 press conference, the leaders of six environmental pressure groups – flanked by Vice President Al Gore and EPA administrator Carol Browner – publicly endorsed NAFTA. Jay Hair (National Wildlife Federation), Peter Berle (National Audubon Society), Kathryn Fuller (WWF), Fred Krupp (EDF), Russell Mittermeier (Conservation International) and John Adams (NRDC) called on Congress to ratify the treaty and the side agreements.[132]

The 'good cop' groups defended NAFTA, whose environment provisions they had helped develop in collaboration with Clinton officials, many of them former colleagues. To a treaty that was supposed to promote free trade, they had managed to add Green protectionism, supranational government agencies and US foreign aid spending.

The 'bad cop' environmental groups continued to oppose NAFTA. They had not participated in the hundreds of meetings at which NAFTA's environmental provisions were drafted. Unmoved by the side agreements, the Sierra Club, Friends of the Earth and Greenpeace denounced the accord, saying it would only enrich giant corporations at the environment's expense. They joined the emerging animal rights movement, labour unions and 'public interest' groups founded by Ralph Nader to lobby against NAFTA.

To Green the GATT

In 1993, parties to the General Agreement on Tariffs and Trade (GATT) began negotiating a new treaty. When it was founded in 1948, GATT was meant to be a non-binding, interim arrangement. The new treaty was supposed to replace the GATT with a permanent World Trade Organisation (WTO), which together with the International Monetary Fund and the World Bank would manage world trade, monetary and employment matters.[133]

Despite their differences, the environmental groups recognised that NAFTA had helped them make inroads in international economic policymaking.

---

[131] Office of the US Trade Representative, 'The NAFTA: Report on Environmental Issues,' *North American Free Trade Agreement Supplemental Agreements and Additional Documents*, (Washington, DC: Government Printing Office, November 1993) p. 14.

[132] Peter Behr, 'For Environmental Groups, Biggest NAFTA Fight is Intramural,' *Washington Post*, September 16, 1993, p. D 10.

[133] William Drozdiak, 'Poor Nations Resist Tougher Trade Rules,' *Washington Post*, April 14, 1994.

Environmental organisations such as the National Wildlife Federation, Greenpeace and WWF to announce their opposition to the GATT talks, but at the same time they lobbied the Administration to negotiate treaty revisions they could support.[134] Environmental groups demanded the following reforms.[135]

- Allow countries to set environmental standards higher than GATT-approved standards, without violating GATT;
- Authorise environmental groups as NGOs to participate in trade disputes: let them file amicus-like briefs and include them as expert consultants to GATT dispute settlement panels;
- Establish an environmental mandate for the GATT: make preparations for a 'Green Round' of global trade negotiations where more elaborate environmental standards could be developed.

Green Audacity Yields Results

The lobbying produced several victories. According to *The GATT Uruguay Round Agreements: A Report on Environmental Issues*, prepared by the US Trade Representative, the Administration acknowledged the influence of green groups and did press for revisions to the negotiating text.[136] When the negotiations were completed on December 15, 1993, the final treaty text showed many signs of their influence:

- Breaking with the existing GATT, the treaty preamble established 'sustainable development' as an objective of the world trade treaty.
- New language tightening environmental standards was inserted. Under the old GATT, such rules had to be 'least trade-restrictive,' meaning they had to hinder trade as little as possible. Under a new World Trade Organisation (WTO), this no longer pertained.
- National governments would have the right to share summaries of trade disputes with NGOs and to provide them with the full text of all government submissions to the new WTO.
- Governments would have the right to provide subsidies to private industry if they promoted environmentalist goals.
- A Committee on Trade and the Environment (CTE) was created in the WTO as a forum to consider additional environmental rules.

Some environmental groups welcomed the WTO, which they anticipated could

---

[134] Timothy Noah, 'Environmental Groups Say Deal Poses Threats,' *Wall Street Journal*, December 16, 1993.
[135] 'Split Among Environmentalists on NAFTA Healed in United Support for GATT Reforms,' *BNA International Environment Daily*, December 7, 1993.
[136] US Trade Representative, *The GATT Uruguay Round Agreements: Report on Environmental Issues*, August 1994, pp. ES-2, 35-40. This report was prepared with the assistance of several cabinet-level agencies participating in the interagency Environmental and Natural Resources Subcommittee of the Trade Policy Staff Committee, the Environmental Protection Agency and the Council on Environmental Quality. The final phase of Uruguay Round negotiations began in late 1992.

become the forum for more environmental regulation of a new system of world trade.

The Developing World Fights Back

The environmental groups issued their Green protectionist demands with the sinking feeling that the WTO would never accept them. Green protectionism was a lost cause at the WTO because the developing countries were on red alert to stop it. Third World leaders were keenly aware that the Green agenda would prevent poor countries from using world trade to expand their economies. Indian Prime Minister P. V. Narasimha Rao rallied the Group of 15 (G-15), a consultative forum for developing countries, against what he called 'attempts to introduce new protectionist agendas'.[137] Rao warned developing countries to 'guard against new trade-restricting tendencies in the developed countries using the pretext of social and environmental concerns'.[138] The G-15 – which included Brazil, Egypt, India, Indonesia, Malaysia, Nigeria and Chile – drafted a common strategy opposing trade-restrictive amendments to the WTO.

'We should not countenance any moves to put social and environmental concerns on the trade agenda, with thinly veiled intentions to nullify the comparative advantage of developing countries,' Rao said in a subsequent UN meeting.[139] Hong Kong, South Korea, Bangladesh and China echoed his position.[140] Malaysia's Prime Minister Mahathir Mohamad said that rich-country trade curbs were designed to deprive the Third World of its only trade advantages – raw materials and lower labour costs. Almost the entire Third World opposed attempts to add an environmental component to the WTO. A G-15 communiqué denounced the Clinton administration's environmental proposals as 'the very antithesis of the principles of free markets and comparative advantage;' it said they would 'create further distortion and inefficiency and undermine growth'.[141]

Still, the US pushed Green protectionism hard. At the April 1994 Marrakech signing ceremony, US Vice President Al Gore lectured Third World delegates that workers' rights and the environment had to be top priorities for the trading system. But representatives of the developing world were just as adamant in opposing the US agenda. Charging that international environmental rules would curtail trade and growth opportunities, their speeches openly attacked NGO-sponsored efforts. India, Brazil and Singapore accused the West of using the vocabulary of environmentalism to disguise trade protectionism, shelter uncompetitive jobs and rob poorer nations of legitimate trading opportunities.[142] The G-15 declined to accept an ambitious Green agenda for the WTO's Committee on Trade and the Environment.

---

[137] N. Vasuki Rao, 'G-15 Leaders Blast Non-Economic Trade Curbs in West,' *Journal of Commerce*, March 29, 1994.

[138] N. Vasuki Rao, 'Developing States to Map Opposition to Trade Curbs,' *Journal of Commerce*, March 31, 1994.

[139] Neelam Jain, 'ESCAP meet in India to discuss GATT,' *United Press International*, April 5, 1994.

[140] 'Fears of US Trade Protectionism Dominating UN Meeting,' *Agence France Presse*, April 7, 1994.

[141] Rao, 'Developing States to Map Opposition to Trade Curbs.'

[142] William Drozdiak, 'Poor Nations Resist Tougher Trade Rules,' *Washington Post*, April 14, 1994.

4. Food Fight: NGO Conflicts over Population Control and Biotechnology

On November 13-17, 1996 the UN's World Food Summit convened in Rome, Italy to plan national and international food policies for the next century. Sponsored by the UN Food and Agriculture Organisation (FAO), the summit was supposed to improve the prospects of 840 million people thought to be suffering from chronic malnutrition. A 'Declaration on World Food Security' and 'Plan of Action' pledged to reduce by half the number of world's hungry by the year 2015.

The conference dealt with many questions that delegates from around the world considered crucial to global 'food security' – agriculture, food marketing and distribution, foreign aid, humanitarian assistance and world trade. But NGO representatives wanted the conference to be organised around the concept of sustainable development. The newspaper headlines might emphasise the distress of the world's hungry, but environment and population control advocacy groups were thinking instead about how to control resource production and consumption. Rather than reduce the number of the world's hungry, their bottom line was controlling the world's population. Mankind's survival was apparently threatened most by life itself – the threat of 'overpopulation.'

The United Nations estimates that by the year 2030 the world's population will increase by three billion people and it frets that there is no way for food production to keep pace. The neo-Malthusians who lobbied delegates to the World Food Summit demanded international action. Regrettably, the FAO sided with them. Officials of the UN agency, which conducts agricultural monitoring and research, forecast that world food production must rise 75 per cent by 2030 just to keep up with the expected increase in population.

The Rome Declaration on Food Security states, 'the problems of hunger and food insecurity have global dimensions and are likely to persist and even increase dramatically in some regions, unless urgent, determined and concerted action is taken, given the anticipated increase in the world's population and the stress on natural resources'.[143] Without the ability to control birth rates, the FAO claimed that governments could not increase agricultural productivity sufficiently to handle the expanding hunger crisis. Representatives of the Worldwatch Institute, an environmental NGO participating in the conference, even went so far as to question the relevance of parts of the Summit Plan of Action if they were not directly linked to population control measures.[144]

Market-based solutions to the problem of hunger were given short shrift. UN Development Programme (UNDP) administrator James Gustave Speth argued that economic liberalisation and private initiative could not deal with the crisis. Speth, a former president of the World Resources Institute and one-time head of President

---

[143] Rome Declaration on Food Security, World Food Summit, 13-17 November, 1996.

[144] Paul Holmes, 'FAO Chief Defends Food Summit as Critics Weigh In,' *Reuters North American Wire*, November 12, 1996.

Carter's Council on Environmental Quality, was responsible for re-orienting UNDP towards sustainable development. He argued that the crisis in food and population required more foreign aid from industrial nations. Said Speth: 'The idea that the private sector can replace development cooperation is a myth'.[145] But for Speth, the most important form of development assistance was preventing Third World people from having children. 'Population stabilisation,' reducing the rate of human population increase, would be the developed world's greatest gift to developing countries.

As at most UN conferences, bold statements by conference organisers disguised widely divergent agendas. The conference's final 'Declaration on World Food Security' affirmed a 'fundamental human right to be free from hunger and malnutrition'.[146] Its 'Plan of Action' – crafted in language purporting to offer the conference's strategic vision – defined food security as access to sufficient amounts of basic food, 'based on healthy and culturally adequate food habits'.[147] This curious definition accommodated a wide range of nutrition concerns. For instance, the US national food security plan identified high-fat diets, lack of exercise and obesity as significant food problems.[148] The plan was developed by the US Department of Agriculture several weeks prior to the conference and it devoted several paragraphs to the problem of over-eating – a strange use of bureaucratic energy for a hunger conference.

Or perhaps, not so strange. The Summit's Plan of Action made clear that food security was simply another aspect of sustainable development. Hence it was related to the special needs of women (the principal issue at the Beijing conference) and population stabilisation (Cairo). It could also relate to the issue of over-consumption by the rich, which sustainable development wants to end. The Plan of Action made it clear that food – whether too little or too much – was tied more to an ideology of resource limitation than to actual pangs of hunger.

Setting the Stage: The 1994 Cairo Conference

The World Food Summit can only be understood in the context of other UN efforts to limit population. The groundwork for the 1996 Rome conference had been laid by the 1994 International Conference on Population and Development in Cairo, Egypt. One hundred and eighty countries attended that UN summit, which was dedicated to holding world population, then 5.67 billion people, under a target level of 7.27 billion by 2015. Governments were supposed to control their populations by spending $17 billion annually on foreign aid and other programmes.

The Cairo conference was dominated less by environmental NGOs than by population control advocates like the International Planned Parenthood Federation. Some environmentalists even complained that the conference was hijacked by the

---

[145] Mahesh Uniyal, 'Food Summit: Pay Up Or Else...' *Inter Press Service*, November 13, 1996.

[146] Rome Declaration on World Food Security, World Food Summit, 13-17 November 1996.

[147] World Food Summit Plan of Action, 13-17 November 1996.

[148] 'The US Contribution to World Food Security: The US Position Paper Prepared for the World Food Summit,' US Department of Agriculture, July 1996.

women's empowerment agenda.[149] The Cairo conference highlighted issues that were considered important in the struggle against overpopulation: women's rights, sex education, reproductive health measures and abortion.

Despite their different emphases, the NGO environmental and population control factions agreed that the world should direct its international agencies and political processes to curtailing childbirths. The environmental movement reasoned that slowing population growth would cut resource use. The Commission on Global Governance, an independent UN advisory group linked to Maurice Strong, doubted 'the capacity of the earth to withstand the impact of human consumption as numbers multiply if present trends of rising economic activity and rising consumption continue unchanged'.[150] Human beings affect the environment in terms of 'what people use and waste,' the Commission asserted. 'Not only population but also consumption has to be reduced if sustainability is to be achieved'. The Commission's report, *Our Global Neighbourhood*, estimated that 'some 80 per cent of what is thought of as prosperity' was actually bad for the planet.[151] Despite what those enjoying it might think, the pleasure of prosperity was ecologically unsustainable.

The Cairo conference on population was defined as a conference on population control and population control was defined in terms of government support for family planning and abortion. This set the stage for international conflict over the foundations of morality. NGO population control proposals – including one proposal to make abortion a basic human right – met fierce resistance in Cairo, not least from Islamic countries. Muslims, who feared the impact of Western immorality on their societies, demonstrated against the conference and urged their leaders to boycott it. The governments of several Islamic countries – Saudi Arabia, Lebanon, Sudan and Niger – were so offended that they did just that.[152]

The Vatican, joined by delegations from predominantly Roman Catholic countries, also opposed many conference proposals. Pope John Paul II condemned what he called the 'culture of death' permeating the policies of many national government programmes and UN agencies. That the Vatican entered a de facto coalition with Muslim authorities demonstrated the extent of their common opposition to rising divorce rates, family decline and deteriorating public mores. Other organisations of religious and social conservatives, some of whom attended the conference, also voiced opposition to its population control measures.[153]

The right to abortion and its role in population control was a key theme at

---

[149] Philip Shabecoff, *A New Name for Peace*, (Hanover, NH: University Press of New England, 1996) p. 181.

[150] Commission on Global Governance, *Our Global Neighbourhood*, (New York: Oxford University Press, 1995) pp . 27-28.

[151] *Our Global Neighbourhood*, p. 145.

[152] Eileen Alt Powell, 'Singing, Canvassing and Lobbying for Family Planning,' *AP Worldstream*, September 2, 1994.

[153] These included Focus on the Family, National Association of Evangelicals, Family Research Council, the Rockford Institute, Catholic Campaign for America, Family of the Americas Foundation, Population Research Institute and Human Life International (Cliff Kincaid, *Global Bondage*, (Lafayette, LA: Huntington House Publishers, 1995) p.99).

Cairo. The United Nations Population Fund, International Planned Parenthood Federation (IPPF), Women's Environment and Development Organisation (WEDO) and allied pro-abortion activists tightly controlled many conference events. The UN attempted to portray the Cairo Conference as the culmination of an open process welcome to NGOs of many backgrounds. A number of NGOs – including the IPPF, the Centre for Reproductive Law and Policy and Catholics for a Free Choice – mounted an unsuccessful effort to strip the Vatican of its UN observer status.[154] Waller also describes an incident in which a journalist was removed from a conference event and almost deported by armed UN police after a member of the National Organisation for Women accused him of being an anti-abortion activist.[155]

Planned Parenthood, an organisation that promotes the universal legalisation of abortion and is supported by corporate manufacturers of contraceptive devices and drugs, such as Norplant, exercised considerable influence over at least 26 delegations from poor countries such as Peru and Bolivia. It offered to pay for IPPF staff and UN employees to represent countries too poor to send delegates to Cairo. IPPF itself had over 200 organisers and lobbyists in Cairo. The US Agency for International Development sent a contingent of 122. The leader of the US delegation, former Colorado senator Tim Wirth, the Under Secretary of State for Global Affairs, was supportive of Planned Parenthood goals; he was once on the board of directors of a Colorado Planned Parenthood affiliate.

By contrast, the Vatican sent a delegation of only seventeen.[156] It tried to counter IPPF tactics in Latin America by asking governments there to put anti-abortion NGOs on their delegations. But of 1,200 NGOs in Cairo, only two dozen were from Catholic and anti-abortion organisations.[157]

Some NGOs from developing countries resented the claim that large families were responsible for poverty. 'The countries of the South reject the main assumption prevailing throughout the Cairo document that population growth in the South is the reason behind poverty and underdevelopment,' their statement said. 'We argue the opposite…The poor will continue to have more children as long they have high infant mortality, lack education, social and health security and need children for labour to support the family'. Instead of government aid for birth control, the group urged that aid be re-directed to combat poverty.[158] (The evidence suggests that wealth and access to financial instruments (such as pensions) is a far more significant factor in determining the number of children a woman has than availability of birth-control measures.)

Other groups from developing countries argued that population control demands were racist. Elida Solorzano, head of the Nicaraguan delegation, said

---

[154] Thalif Deen, 'Population-Religion: NGOs Set Sights on Holy See's UN Status,' *Inter Press Service*, September 6, 1994.

[155] John Michael Waller, 'Bella's Babies, *American Spectator*, April 1995.

[156] Ibid.

[157] George Moffett, 'UN Population Conference Meets Religious Resistance,' *Christian Science Monitor*, September 6, 1994.

[158] *Agence France Presse*, 'It's Poverty that Causes Population Boom, Not Other Way Round: NGOs,' September 12, 1994.

Western population controllers 'don't want any more dark people multiplying, we know that'. Third World community workers complained that UN-supplied health centres in their countries lacked antibiotics, but were plentiful in condoms, pills and intra-uterine devices. Kenyan paediatrician Margaret Ologa explained, 'We are running out of vaccine. We have no syringes, no needles, no sulpha drugs, no penicillin. Yet our Family Welfare Centres never lack birth-control supplies'.[159] Health workers from the Philippines and Tanzania said they were not warned that some contraceptives can have dangerous side-effects, such as haemorrhaging, permanent sterility and other injuries.[160]

The 1994 Cairo conference gave population controllers the conference document they wanted – the 'Plan of Action.' Rumours had circulated among Third World country delegations that US State Department officials were threatening to cut off foreign aid funding unless they voted for the Plan of Action.[161] The Vatican and Islamic countries were forced to accept watered-down language on 'reproductive rights,' which could be interpreted to suit the UN and its IPPF allies.

NGOs Call the Shots

The 1996 World Food Summit gave population and environment NGOs another chance to organise their forces. The Clinton administration worked closely with them, as State Department Under-secretary Wirth and his deputy Melinda Kimble made sure that even the radical fringe of the movement was intimately involved in crafting US policy. The Administration relied heavily on the opinions of Dianne Dillon-Ridgley, president of Zero Population Growth (ZPG) and appointed her to the US delegation to Rome.[162] It also took its signals from Lester Brown, founder of the Worldwatch Institute and another prominent Administration adviser. Wirth publicly commended Brown for helping craft the federal government's policy positions.[163] (In late 1997 Wirth left State to manage media mogul Ted Turner's $1 billion foundation, which will fund UN environment and population initiatives.)

The NGO outlook figured prominently in the US Position Paper that the Agriculture Department prepared for the World Food Summit. This lengthy document surveys recent scholarly projections of future world food supply and demand. Yet it takes seriously the predictions contained in the Worldwatch volume *Full House: Reassessing the Earth's Population Carrying Capacity* (1994) by Brown and Hal Kane. Brown and Kane say that in the food sector, 'human demands are colliding with some of the earth's limits'. Ecological constraints are starting to slow the growth of food production, such that 'food security will replace

---

[159] Waller, 'Bella's Babies.'

[160] *Inter Press Service*, 'Population-Contraceptives: Problems of the Poor and Uninformed,' September 12, 1994.

[161] Eileen Alt Powell, 'Singing, Canvassing and Lobbying for Family Planning,' *AP Worldstream*, September 2, 1994.

[162] Other NGO representatives included C. Payne Lucas, President, Africare; Charles MacCormack, President & CEO, Save the Children; Leland Swenson, President, National Farmers Union. Private Sector Advisors to the US Delegation to the World Food Summit as of 10/15/96.

[163] World Food Summit public briefing, US Department of Agriculture, October 17, 1996 (attended by author).

military security as the principal preoccupation of national governments'. They also repeat earlier predictions of doom that never materialised: 'Over the next 40 years, the world will face massive grain deficits in Africa, the Indian subcontinent and China'.[164] The US government position paper side-steps the truth of the statements and credits the authors by advising that 'regardless of their validity...Brown's analyses offer an important warning against becoming complacent about the future food situation'.[165]

While official delegates to the Summit were meeting, NGO representatives conducted a separate forum courtesy of the Italian Foreign Affairs Ministry, which provided $320,000 in funding.[166] This gave the over 1,500 NGO participants somewhat less power than they enjoyed at the Habitat II conference in Istanbul, where NGO delegates directly participated in official negotiations. Yet it afforded participants an opportunity 'to do some strategic planning for campaigns we are working on,' in the words of Susan Davis, executive director of WEDO.[167]

The Path to Rome

Direct NGO involvement in World Food Summit deliberations was limited to input provided at five earlier regional conferences. Held in Morocco, Burkina Faso, Israel, Thailand and Paraguay and sponsored by the FAO, these allowed NGOs such as Oxfam, Christian Aid and Action Aid to inject their views into the process that would produce the final text of the Summit's key documents, the Rome Declaration and Plan of Action. They insisted on more foreign assistance for population control – and offered themselves as administrative conduits to give vent to their passions.[168]

Just before the Summit, the FAO invited more than 200 NGOs to Rome on September 19-21, 1996 for yet another 'consultation session.' This meeting became a rallying point for proponents of 'sustainable agriculture,' representatives of peasants and indigenous peoples, advocates for consumers, the urban poor, children's rights and fair trade and feminists and AIDS activists.[169] The NGOs used the session as a platform to criticise the market system on the grounds that it 'generates exclusion and poverty and is not conducive to attaining equitable and sustainable development, social justice and gender equality'.[170] Needless to say they did not support this contention with any reliable evidence.

NGO and Government Paths Diverge

The NGOs present at the earlier consultation session were in no mood to

---

[164] Lester Brown and Hal Kane, *Full House: Reassessing the Earth's Population Carrying Capacity*, (New York: Norton, 1994).

[165] 'The US Contribution to World Food Security: The US Position Paper Prepared for the World Food Summit,' US Department of Agriculture, July 1996.

[166] Ibid.

[167] C. Gerald Fraser, 'NGOs: Using the Summit to Organise Campaigns,' *Earth Times*, November 16-30, 1996.

[168] Regional conference reports available at http://www.fao.org/wfs/resource/resource.htm.

[169] Committee on World Food Security, Twenty-second Session Rome, 23 – 27 September 1996, FAO/NGO Consultation on the World Food Summit, (19-21 September 1996): Key Points of the Consultation.

[170] FAO/NGO Consultation on the World Food Summit, (19-21 September 1996).

procrastinate when they arrived at the Food Summit. Delegates said a draft of the Plan of Action did not go far enough. The Plan implied that hunger was a fault of governments' unwillingness to guarantee human rights, but it carefully declined to endorse an explicit 'right to food,' not wanting to impose a legal obligation on governments.

Fearing such a new right would give US citizens legal standing to sue the federal government, the US delegation filed a reservation so that 'right to food' claims could not be legally binding. The US delegation announced that it accepted the Rome Declaration but noted that it would not lead to 'any change in the current state of conventional or customary international law'.[171] Administration officials carefully explained that no right to food was in the US Constitution and they took exception to the UN proposal that Western governments target 0.7 per cent of their national wealth for foreign aid. They did promise that the US would strive to guarantee freedom from hunger through 'empowerment' programmes.

The NGOs were displeased. More than 1,200 agrarian and development aid groups from 80 countries complained that the Rome Plan of Action was inadequate. Their list of alternatives included demands for higher subsidies to small farmers and the promotion of ecological farming practices.[172] On the last day of the Summit, NGO protesters shouted 'farce' and heckled the UN's FAO director-general Jacques Diouf of Senegal.[173]

Clash over Population Control

If the United States was the most powerful and outspoken government advocate for population control, its primary opponent was the Roman Catholic Church. As at Cairo, the Vatican refuted claims that overpopulation was the major cause of world hunger. In an address to the conference, Pope John Paul II declared, 'Populations on their own don't imply food shortages and we must do away with the sophistry that if we are numerous then we are condemned to be poor'. The Pontiff appealed to the delegates: 'Arbitrary stabilisation, or even reduction, of population will not solve the problem of hunger'.[174] Eleven Islamic countries joined the Vatican in filing reservations to the Summit Plan of Action. (A country declares provisions non-binding when it files a reservation.) They objected to language on sexual and reproductive rights and family planning, terms they regarded as favourable to abortion.

The NGOs rejected these countries' message and left little doubt about their own agenda. 'Although scientifically, there is no proof that we cannot feed all the people in the world, in reality it just will not happen,' said Ingar Brueggemann,

---

[171] Michael Adler, 'World Food Summit Left Key Issues Unresolved,' *Agence France Presse*, November 18, 1996.

[172] Deutsche Presse-Agentur, November 17, 1996

[173] Paul Holmes, 'UN Food Summit Ends Under Shadow of Disagreements,' *Reuters North American Wire*, November 17, 1996.

[174] Dipankar De Sarkar, 'Food Summit: Pope Declares Overpopulation Not the Problem,' *Inter Press Service*, November 13, 1996.

Secretary General of the International Planned Parenthood Foundation (IPPF).[175] The pro-abortion NGOs fell back on the mantra-like assertion: countries must not 're-open' questions that were settled in Cairo. The 1994 population conference documents are virtually etched in stone and countries ought not to upset the continuity of subsequent UN summits.

In a report on the Summit, the anti-abortion group Human Life International (HLI) accused IPPF and the UN Fund for Population Activities of 'spreading misery throughout the world, especially in unsuspecting developing nations in the guise of 'family planning''.[176] HLI, Concerned Women for America and other anti-abortion organisations were shut out of the UN proceedings even though they had obtained 'NGO status,' which ought to have afforded them access to the plenary session and enabled them to speak with delegates. The UN revoked their NGO privileges at the last minute and eleven women from anti-abortion groups in six nations protested this exclusion at a press conference.[177]

Gathering Clouds

Despite their massive presence in Rome, the NGOs were troubled by the direction of the Food Summit. The agenda sometimes seemed outside their control and they suspected that multinational corporations had hijacked it. Official summit delegates appeared not to focus solely on population and gender equality, but also discussed the Uruguay Round trade agreement in favourable terms. WEDO's Davis concluded, 'This summit became a food trade summit rather than a food security summit as the trade negotiators were almost all the same people who were going to Singapore [for the World Trade Organisation meeting in December]'.[178]

The NGOs feared that Third World agriculture was vulnerable to the logic of the marketplace. They insisted that poverty is caused by the unequal distribution of wealth, inequitable trade between developed and developing countries and flawed macroeconomic policies. They urged developed countries to meet the UN foreign aid goal of 0.7 per cent of gross domestic product (GDP).[179] They called for 'sustainable agriculture,' the term for farming without the chemicals, pesticides and fertilisers that enable increased crop yields on fewer acres.[180] They denounced any expression of interest in biotechnology and accused Western corporations of exploiting and polluting the genetic resources of developing countries. Corporations that tried to increase agricultural productivity by manipulating plant genes stood accused of tampering with nature for profit.[181] Instead, the NGOs championed 'farmers' rights' and supported subsidies and other benefits for ecologically sound farming by members of local indigenous communities.

---

[175] Dipankar De Sarkar, 'Population: NGO Slams Pope's Food Summit Message,' *Inter Press Service*, December 2, 1996.

[176] De Sarkar, 'Population: NGO Slams Pope's Food Summit Message.'

[177] 'Pro-Family Group Silenced at FAO Summit,' press release, Concerned Women for America, November 15, 1996.

[178] De Sarkar, 'Population: NGO Slams Pope's Food Summit Message.'

[179] Jorge Pina, 'Development: Foreign Debt Question Divides North and South,' *Inter Press Service*, September 28, 1996.

[180] Dave Juday, 'The UN's Food Fight,' *The Weekly Standard*, November 25, 1996, p. 20.

[181] Dipankar De Sarkar, 'Agriculture: Rich-Poor Clash Looms at FAO Conference,' *Inter Press Service*, June 17, 1996.

In Rome five protesters – including three naked women with anti-American slogans painted across their bodies – disrupted a news conference by US Agriculture Secretary Dan Glickman to publicise their opposition to biotechnology. They accused US agribusiness of importing genetically modified (GM) seed hybrids, undercutting local producers in Europe and threatening the viability if European agriculture.[182] The protesters claimed that GM seed hybrids are dangerous, despite the fact that following stringent tests government agencies in the US and Europe had declared them safe.

The Campaign Against Biotechnology

The Green attacks on GM crops have accelerated since the World Food Summit. Jeremy Rifkin, founder of Earth First! (a group that advocates eco-terrorism) and the guru of the anti-technology movement, frets that biotechnology will produce 'a form of annihilation every bit as deadly as nuclear holocaust'.[183]

The issue has become particularly volatile in Europe, where Greenpeace is at the forefront of a campaign against GM foods.[184] Switzerland's Ciba-Geigy, for instance, has developed a new variety of corn that is resistant to a pest known as the corn borer. But environmental groups ignore these benefits and focus exclusively on various improbable impacts.

Monsanto has been attacked for engineering a soybean that resists one of its own herbicides (Roundup), an innovation that results in lower herbicide use and higher productivity. But in November 1996 five Greenpeace protesters were arrested in Louisiana for disrupting a Cargill grain-loading terminal where Monsanto soybeans were being transported by ship. Using inflatable rafts, the Greenpeace activists posted yellow signs on two ships that read 'X-Genetic Experiment.' Other Greenpeace protesters, wearing white hats and blue overalls labelled 'Genetic Experiment,' chained themselves to gates and grain barges at the Archer Daniels Midland grain terminal in Louisiana, protesting exports of genetically modified soybeans.[185] Greenpeace also blockaded ports in Antwerp and Ghent, Belgium that were receiving soybean imports from Cargill [186] as well as targeting food companies, including Unilever, Danone and Nestlé, in nine European countries to prevent the sale of foods enhanced by biotechnology.

The business community recognises the seriousness of the activist anti-biotech campaign, fearing it will mislead the public. 'The commercial interests in the business, particularly in Germany, are nervous about the effects Greenpeace and their small band of activists can have on the oilseed markets,' reports Jim Hershey of the American Soybean Association.[187]

The Convention on Biological Diversity (CBD), which was negotiated at the

[182] Philip Pullella, 'Food Summit Opens with Appeal for Zaire,' *Washington Times*, (Reuters), November 14, 1996.

[183] Quoted in Henry I. Miller, 'Techno-bashers Distortions Are Hurting Earth Day,' *Houston Chronicle*, April 22, 1997.

[184] Control Risks Group Ltd., *No Hiding Place: Business and the Politics of Pressure*, July 1997, pp.23 -26.

[185] *Reuters North American Wire*, 'Greenpeace Activists Arrested for Blocking Grain Terminal,' November 14, 1996.

[186] *Reuters European Community Report*, 'US Greenpeace Activists Arrested in Biotech Soy Protest,' November 21, 1996.

[187] *Reuters Financial Report*, 'ASA, Monsanto Take Greenpeace Protests Seriously,' September 20, 1996.

1992 Rio summit, is one device that the environmental movement intends to use to exploit fears of biotechnology. The CBD contains a Biosafety Protocol that proposes the development of international biotechnology regulations under which, 'No one anywhere would be allowed to grow and test a biotechnology derived crop or garden plant – even on a plot as small as one-tenth of an acre – without prior approval from the UN bio-police'.[188]

The biotech scares are false. Advances in biotechnology promise a new 'Green Revolution' in agricultural production, delivering even more benefits in high-yielding crop varieties, pest-resistant hybrids and other genetic innovations. In the Third World, six million square miles of cropland today feed twice as many people as was possible in 1960. Because of agricultural productivity there are no signs of imminent world famine, despite environmentalist predictions. Where famine does occur, the cause is not a failure in productivity, but one of political will and judgement.[189]

Unfortunately, international environmental organisations hostility to new technology has had consequences for developing nations. 'Extremist environmentalists' opposed to chemical fertilisers, pesticides and GM crops now threaten Africa's ability to grow more food. That is the recent warning of Dr. Norman Borlaug, winner of the 1970 Nobel Peace Prize for the pioneering scientific work that made possible the 'Green Revolution' in Third World agriculture. Borlaug warns that opponents of biotechnology actually increase the likelihood of environmental degradation. By preventing the use of fertilisers, pesticides and GM crops to increase crop yield, they will force farmers to convert forest and mountain lands to cropland of marginal productivity. [190]

Borlaug speaks from experience: when he tried to bring the latest agricultural technologies to Africa in the 1980s, the environmental movement pressed the World Bank and the Ford Foundation to refuse funding for high-yield farming methods, claiming that these techniques would destroy the environment and arguing that more food would merely stimulate population growth, which they see as evil in itself.[191]

Despite the influence of the Malthusian environmental lobby, most Third World countries appear to be rejecting their gloom and doom message. Compared with earlier UN conferences, the NGOs participating in the Rome World Food Summit lost ground. The official delegates focused their attention on a wider range of issues than grim warnings about sustainability. Perhaps that's because Third World governments know that their economic futures depend on freer trade and modern agriculture, not cultural isolation and ecologically restricted farming. The important role of religion in the developing world also suggests that governments will hesitate to impose population and farming restrictions on their people.

---

[188] Henry I. Miller, 'Harming the Environment,' *Journal of Commerce*, July 31, 1997.
[189] Juday, 'The UN's Food Fight.'
[190] Gene Kramer, *Associated Press*, 'Nobel Laureate Favours Fertiliser,' August 4, 1997.
[191] Gregg Easterbrook, 'Forgotten Benefactor of Humanity: Agronomist Norman Borlaug,' *Atlantic Monthly*, January 1997.

6. Seeing green at the World Bank

The World Bank is an international lending institution that finances economic development projects in the Third World. Founded in 1944, it disbursed $20 billion to 241 projects in Latin America, Eastern Europe, Asia and Africa in 1997. The US government provides roughly one-fifth of the World Bank's funding. Other Western governments and Japan contribute the rest. Environmental advocacy groups are well aware that these funds give the World Bank an enormous influence over the economies of borrower nations. They rightly conclude that it is often more effective for them to lobby the World Bank than to lobby foreign governments.

At one time environmental pressure groups organised picket lines outside the World Bank's Washington, DC headquarters. They were eager to denounce Bank lending projects because they considered them environmentally dangerous, but over the past decade environmental lobbyists have adopted a new role. They have become counsellors to the World Bank and conduits for its lending. NGOs remain critical of many World Bank loans, but as they become distributors and beneficiaries of Bank grant-making, they have grown more prudent in their criticisms and more understanding of the Bank's problems.

In the past decade NGO-World Bank collaboration has increased and become institutionalised. In 1997, NGOs participated in nearly 50 per cent of all Bank projects.[192] Often these were so-called 'development NGOs' that provide direct services with World Bank funds – private voluntary organisations such as Red Cross societies and refugee relief organisations such as Oxfam and Save the Children Fund. They were involved in 81 per cent of the Bank's agriculture projects, 60 per cent of its health and population programmes and 69 per cent of other social sector projects.

Environmental advocacy groups are also major participants in Bank projects. Indeed, environmental pressure groups have won an extraordinary influence over Bank lending policies in a short time. Environmental NGOs were active in the twelve Bank environmental sector projects undertaken in 1997. Although only five per cent of its projects are in the environmental sector, the Bank's record of lending is impressive. By 1997, the World Bank had extended $11.6 billion in cumulative loans for environmental projects, up from $1.9 billion in 1990.193 It is possible that the transformation of NGOs from fierce Bank critics into sympathetic collaborators may be related to their appreciation of the Bank's capacity for generous spending.[194]

The World Bank's History of Failed Reform

In the early 1980s environmental groups were valuable critics of World Bank operations. Even as Third World governments eagerly lined up for Bank funding,

---

[192] *World Bank Annual Report 1997*, p. 16.

[193] *World Bank Annual Report 1997*, p. 24.

[194] In 1997, the World Bank spent $832.6 million on its staff, $119.5 million on consultants and $126 million on travel. (*World Bank Annual Report 1997*, Washington DC: World Bank, 1997, p. 159.)

NGOs argued that its loans were too often spent on large and poorly-conceived projects. Often these were massive construction projects that forced the resettlement of tens of thousands of people, destroyed local communities and violated human rights. The NGOs pointed out that Bank financing for economic development was actually perpetuating poverty and environmental despoliation.

NGOs often cite Brazil's Polonoroeste project in regional development and agricultural colonisation as a demonstration of how World Bank financing produces ruin. This colossal example of central planning envisioned bringing a vast area of the Amazon rainforest into agricultural cultivation. It also proposed an extensive road building programme to connect the project to populated areas of the nation.[195] NGOs charged that $443 million in World Bank loans produced catastrophic effects by introducing slash-and-burn agricultural practices, the loans subsidising the rapid deforestation of the Amazon basin. The project even helped spread malaria from the Amazon region to more populous parts of Brazil.

The director of Canada's Probe International, an environmental group, documented the Bank's role in a 1991 book, Odious Debts. Patricia Adams condemned the impact of Polonoroeste: 'Indian lands are systematically seized, generally without compensation and Indian economies destroyed,' she wrote. 'The livelihoods of non-Indian dwellers – mainly rubber tappers who for generations had collected rubber, Brazil nuts and rainforest products – are also threatened'.[196]

Bruce Rich, a programme officer at the Environmental Defence Fund (EDF), agreed. His book Mortgaging the Earth describes Polonoroeste as 'an unprecedented ecological and human calamity'.[197] Rich also described other unfortunate Bank loans. One $770 million development loan to Indonesia was intended to create enough economic opportunities to prompt two and one-half million impoverished people to migrate to more remote parts of the nation. But the project failed, producing more deforestation than jobs and generating only more human misery.

Confronting reports of abuses such as these, groups such as EDF, the Natural Resources Defence Council, the Environmental Policy Institute, National Wildlife Federation and the Sierra Club petitioned Congress for relief. In 1983, environmental groups and Indian tribes testified before a congressional committee against the Bank, which answered with a forty-eight page memo attempting to refute their charges. The Bank assured Congress that it would not repeat its mistakes and warned that the environmentalist testimony 'may create the misleading impression that past trends continue'.[198]

The World Bank worked hard to neutralise environmental critics. Bank president A.W. Clausen, a former head of Bank of America, met with

---

[195] Patricia Adams, *Odious Debts: Loose Lending, Corruption and the Third World's Environmental Legacy*, (London: Earthscan 1991) pp. 28-31.
[196] Adams, p. 30.
[197] Bruce Rich, *Mortgaging the Earth: The World Bank, Environmental Impoverishment and the Crisis of Development*, (Boston: Beacon Press, 1994) p. 27.
[198] World Bank, *'Response to Statements of Environmental Organisations, Sent by the US Executive Director'* (Washington, DC, World Bank, unpublished, January 11, 1984), p.1, cited in Rich, *Mortgaging the Earth*, p. 337 at note 26.

environmental leaders and asked them not to lobby against Bank funding. He said the Bank was amending its operations manual and would no longer finance projects that degraded the environment or forced human resettlement. The Greens acquiesced and merely lobbied Congress to require the Bank to increase its environmental staff, share information with NGOs and support smaller, less destructive projects.

Environmentalist fortunes further improved in 1986 when New York's Barber Conable, a senior Republican member of the House of Representatives, succeeded Clausen. With the world press reporting on the failure of many loan projects, Conable's mission was to restore the Bank's credibility and convince his former colleagues that the institution deserved continued taxpayer support. Shortly after taking office, Conable launched an aggressive Bank reorganisation and began soliciting the views of environmental NGOs. Groups such as the World Resources Institute submitted lists of complaints and an agenda of reforms.

The Conable reforms did not markedly improve Bank performance. A 1992 internal review determined that 37 per cent of the Bank's 1991 projects were unsatisfactory. According to the Bank's own criteria, they were failing to produce benefits. The review, conducted by then-Bank vice president Willi Wapenhans, attributed deterioration of the loan portfolio to the Bank's deep-rooted financial problems, including a 'systematic and growing bias towards excessive optimistic rate of return expectations at appraisal'. Wapenhans described borrower nations' failure to comply with financial loan covenants as 'gross and overwhelming'.[199] The Conable reforms had no real impact.

Environmentalist frustrations and criticisms mounted. By 1992 the left-wing Friends of the Earth and the NGO Development Group for Alternative Policies (Development GAP) had organised 'Fifty Years is Enough.' This referred to the upcoming fiftieth anniversary of Bretton Woods, the conference that created the World Bank, the International Monetary Fund (IMF) and the General Agreement on Tariffs and Trade (GATT), the modern institutions of the world economic order. Convinced that the Bank was too eager to lend money for 'development' at the expense of the environment, a campaign spokesman flatly declared, 'The Bank has done more damage than good'.[200]

Anti-Bank NGOs then announced their opposition to continued US funding for the International Development Association (IDA). This was the World Bank's sizeable 'soft loan window,' which provides low-interest subsidised loans for poor countries. The Environmental Defence Fund, Friends of the Earth, Greenpeace and the Sierra Club announced that the 'tenth replenishment' of IDA – the tenth successive appropriation of US tax dollars for the Association – would further degrade the world's environment without alleviating world poverty. Said Lori

---

[199] Portfolio Management Task Force, 'Effective Implementation: Key to Development Impact,' Report No. 92-195, World Bank, Washington, DC, November 3, 1992.
[199] Clay Chandler, 'The Growing Urge to break the Bank,' *Washington Post*, June 19, 1994.
[200] Clay Chandler, 'The Growing Urge to break the Bank,' *Washington Post*, June 19, 1994.

Udall, an attorney with the Environmental Defence Fund, 'At this point in time we don't believe the World Bank can be trusted to use taxpayers' money in a responsible manner which helps the poor and the environment in developing countries. Along with our counterparts in borrower and donor countries, we are launching a worldwide campaign to reduce funding to the World Bank'.[201]

The NGO mobilisation against 'IDA-10' was made more urgent by the drama of the Narmada Dam, a World Bank-financed project in India. Environmental and development organisations and human rights activists joined forces against the massive water project. They claimed the dam, also known as the Sardar Sarovar project, would cause the involuntary resettlement of 200,000 people. They also publicised human rights abuses alleged by local villagers protesting the project and World Bank involvement. By 1993, anti-Narmada forces had generated so much unfavourable publicity that the government of India cancelled the project. Jubilant environmentalists saw Narmada as a model for future campaigns and looked forward to a chain reaction of World Bank loan cancellations. 'Clearly the World Bank is not an institution that can be trusted to use American taxpayers' money wisely in developing countries,' said EDF.[202]

More than fifty organisations, including Oxfam and Greenpeace, joined 'Fifty Years is Enough.' In 1994, the campaign staged a sit-in at an official press conference in Madrid, Spain for the Bretton Woods fiftieth anniversary celebration. Other protest activities followed. The campaign, said one commentator, caused the Bank and the IMF to suffer 'the worst loss of reputation in their history'.[203]

This steady drumbeat of NGO pressure yielded further World Bank reform efforts. But US-based NGOs contended that the World Bank was incapable of reforming itself. Despite years of lobbying and the promise of reforms initiated by Conable and his successor, Lewis Preston, environmental groups concluded that the Bank's decision-making was driven by an internal bureaucratic imperative to loan billions of dollars.

For more than a decade, citizens' groups in the United States, in collaboration with partner organisations in the Third World and Eastern Europe, have lobbied the IMF and the World Bank, as well as the US government, for reforms in their operations and policies. Despite these efforts and the growing chorus of criticism from the US Congress, governments and UN agencies, the IMF and World Bank continue to resist fundamental and meaningful change.

Lori Udall in 1994 congressional testimony[204]

---

[201] Environmental Defence Fund, 'EDF Calls For US Funding to World Bank to be Cut Dramatically,' *EDF News Release*, October 26, 1992.
[202] Environmental Defence Fund, 'World Bank To Cancel Loan To Narmada Dam In India: EDF Calls World Bank Environmental And Social Record Dismal,' *EDF News Release*, March 30, 1993.
[203] Cleary, p. 89.
[204] Testimony of Lori Udall, Director, International Rivers Network on behalf of the Fifty Years is Enough Campaign,

Writer John Thibodeau of Canada's Probe International pronounced the Bank reforms 'resounding failures'. His study, 'The World Bank's Persisting Failure to Reform', excoriated management failings over a ten-year period. It claimed the Bank was intent on burying its critics in paper, 'adding new policies and practices, producing new handbooks and guidelines for staff and undertaking review after review, all intended to address the ill-effects of its lending'.[205] The Probe report wondered whether the Bank could be reformed at all. Probe urged donor governments to 'halt future appropriations of their constituents' scarce tax dollars to this flawed institution'.

Enter Wolfensohn

In 1995 a new president took charge of the World Bank. James Wolfensohn was a prominent Wall Street investment banker and a protégé of Maurice Strong, the UN's top advisor on reform. A champion of wildlife and habitat, Wolfensohn quickly became an outspoken critic of Bank projects that he considered dangerous to the natural environment. Early in his tenure, he cancelled the Arun dam, a major $175 million construction project in Nepal.

Wolfensohn's sheer activism also helped ease NGO pressures on the Bank He met frequently with local NGOs on his travels to World Bank borrower nations in Eastern Europe and the Third World. At the World Bank's 1995 annual meeting, Wolfensohn held a joint press conference with three development NGOs – Forum of African Voluntary Development Organisations, Oxfam International and InterAction – where he urged the US to increase its Bank funding.[206]

In 1997 the Bank began making the first in a series of loans to implement the anticipated Kyoto global warming treaty. Intended to promote development while protecting the environment, the loans are meant to be a model for future World Bank lending. 'My reading is that the Bank is clearly moving in the right direction,' says Robert Watson, director of the World Bank's environment department.[207] Watson is himself a token of environmental concern; he is an atmospheric scientist who has worked for years in the federal government promoting the ozone hole and global warming scares.

Yet James Wolfensohn's promises and actions only repeat the tactics of A.W. Clausen, Barber Conable and Lewis Preston. An April 1997 internal Bank review of 150 projects concluded that his reforms were not going well. The Bank's internal culture of rapid loan approval had not been slowed, nor was there any speed-up in the cancellation of non-performing loans.[208]

The Bank cannot trim its staff while initiating the far-reaching social and environmental reviews demanded by the NGOs. Caught between political

Senate Appropriations Committee, Subcommittee on Foreign Operations, May 17,1994.
[205] Ibid.
[206] *FY96 Progress Report*, p. 22.
[207] Jeremy Peolfsky, 'It's a Small Lender, After All: World Bank Shifts Focus to Leaner, More Ecologically Sound Projects,' Bloomberg News, *The Gazette* (Montreal), September 11, 1997, Pg. D5.
[208] Bruce Stokes, 'Wolfensohn's World,' *National Journal*, Vol. 29, No. 38, September 20, 1997 p. 1846.

crosscurrents, the quality of Bank projects continues to languish. 'It's fair to say that the bank has launched some new environmental initiatives,' comments Andrea Durbin, director of international programmes at Friends of the Earth. However, 'the implementation has been slow and sometimes doesn't happen, (and) the over-all portfolio hasn't shifted significantly'.[209]

In 1997, a Centre for Strategic and International Studies task force concluded that the Bank had failed to reform its lending processes, overhaul its bureaucratic structure and achieve transparency and accountability to outside review. The report described the Bank as 'adept at keeping outsiders from differentiating between public relations pronouncements and real changes in bank activities'.[260]

The Money Tree

Will the NGOs now follow through on their severe criticisms? Will they force reform by lobbying to de-fund multilateral lenders? A few groups such as Canada's Probe International will go that far, but most will not. Development NGOs in Europe and the Third World are particularly reluctant to sanction cuts in US funding. Their food aid and disaster relief programmes depend on US government subsidies. But many environmental lobby groups also have a diminishing interest in fighting the World Bank. In 1996, World Bank direct grants to NGOs totalled $36.8 million. The Bank's annual report, however, shows that it made $105.3 million in direct contributions to the Special Grants Programme.[210] These grants have given the environmental lobby and other NGOs an enormous incentive to keep quiet whenever it is time for Congress to approve the World Bank budget.

The World Bank provides no public accounting of how much of its lending actually benefits NGOs. Some grant money goes directly to NGOs for studies and consultations. Typically, however, a foreign government will request Bank funding for a project. But the grant is usually administered by one or more NGOs acting on the government's behalf.[211] In theory, the NGOs are paid consultants or contractors to the government receiving the loan. In practice, they often run the show.

Social Funds

In Latin America and Africa, the Bank has apportioned over $1 billion cumulatively to some 30 'social funds' that it has established to pay for particular projects involving NGOs. For instance, the World Bank gave $2.3 million to the Planned Parenthood Association of Ghana to pay for programmes to prevent childbearing and population growth.[212] The Bolivian Emergency Social Fund paid

---

[209] Peolfsky, Ibid.

[260] Abid Aslam 'Finance: Development Banks Seen lagging on Reform, Inter Press Service, September 19, 1997.

[210] *World Bank Annual Report 1997*, p. 159.

[211] World Bank, Operations Policy Department, *Working with NGOs; A Practical Guide to Operational Collaboration Between The World Bank and Non-governmental Organisations*, March 1995, p. 47.

[212] *Working with NGOs*, p. 48.

NGOs for what it termed 'long term development activities.'[213] Clearly, NGOs face great temptation to engage in self-dealing. When NGO representatives sit on World Bank social fund boards that decide how monies are distributed; when they serve on social fund committees that design, select and evaluate projects; and when they help borrower governments administer social funds, there will be many opportunities to enhance the NGO role.[214]

Special Grants Programme

This World Bank programme typically gives NGOs between $200,000 to $2 million per grant. The unclear purpose of this programme is to help NGOs participate in the 'development process.' Funds from the programme have been used to cover travel expenses for NGO representatives to attend such UN meetings as the Population Conference in Cairo, the World Summit on Social Development in Copenhagen and the Women's Conference in Beijing.[265] By subsidising NGO travel, the World Bank gives UN conferences the appearance of broad public support. In fact, the NGOs receiving travel benefits are selected because they endorse UN objectives. In 1996, NGOs received a total of $5.34 million through this programme.

In 1996, NGOs also received $800,000 through the Safe Motherhood Special Grants Programme for 'maternal health advocacy research and interventions,'[266] and $850,000 through the Population NGOs Special Grants Programme to promote 'demand creation' for abortion, contraception and sterilisation.[267] Grants programmes also supported NGO conferences, seminars and networking activities (e.g., a women's leadership seminar in India, a small business workshop in the Philippines, a conference on environmental problems in the Black Sea).215 Another $10 million was budgeted in 1997 for the Project in Support of NGOs in West Bank/Gaza.216

Small Grants Programme

In 1996, the Bank gave out $600,000 in small grants of between $10,000 and $15,000 to 'promote dialogue and dissemination of information about international development'. In 1997, $700,000 went to 60 organisations. Programme grants support 'conferences, seminars, publications, networking activities and other information-related activities'.217 The programme gave $15,000 to a Honduran

---

[213] World Bank, Participation and NGO Group, Poverty and Social Policy Department, *The World Bank's Partnership with Non-governmental Organisations*, (Washington DC: World Bank, May 1996) *The World Bank's Partnership with Non-governmental Organisations*, p.8.

[214] World Bank, NGO Group, Social Development Department, 'Cooperation Between the World Bank and NGOs,' *FY96 Progress Report*, August 1997, p. 14.

[265] The World Bank's Partnership with Non-governmental Organisations, p. 10.

[266] *Working with NGOs*, p. 49.

[267] *FY96 Progress Report*, p. 14.

[215] *The World Bank's Partnership with Non-governmental Organisations*, p.11.

[216] *FY96 Progress Report*, p.15.

[217] *FY96 Progress Report*, p.14.

NGO for a conference to discuss the initial results of a Green Manure Technology Kit. It provided $9,000 to Conservation Asia, an NGO in Nepal, to facilitate 'networking on environmental issues'. The Lorma Community Development Foundation received $13,000 for NGO caucuses to lobby the Philippine government.218 Another $15,000 went to a Brazilian NGO to participate in the June 1997 Rio+5 conference on the results of the 1992 Earth Summit. The programme is a slush fund for NGO planning.[219]

Global Environment Facility

Many World Bank subsidies to NGOs are delivered through programmes such as the Global Environment Facility. The GEF is a lending agency to support the goals of the Climate Change and Biodiversity conventions, among others. The World Bank and the United Nations jointly run it. By 1994, NGOs had received a cumulative total of $10 million from the GEF to promote the UN's global warming agenda as well as to implement land use controls in the Third World.220 The US government funds GEF activities even though the US Senate has not ratified the Biodiversity convention.

What Do NGOs Want?

When environmental NGOs opposed World Bank lending, they helped stymie the financial and environmental mismanagement of borrower governments, the proximate cause of decades of Third World stagnation. NGO lobbying also reduced the foreign aid burden of American taxpayers.

But environmental NGOs now refuse to take the final step. They oppose attempts in Congress to reduce or end US funding of the World Bank. EDF's Bruce Rich, who literally 'wrote the book' on the World Bank's environmental devastation, has gone strangely soft. 'Cuts in funding will be the greatest spur to reform,' he wrote in 1994. 'It is the only external pressure that World Bank management appears to take really seriously'.[271] Yet one year later, Rich's tone was radically different: 'There is clearly a role for such an institution, but the Bank must focus on quality rather than quantity in its lending'. Rich deemed the Bank's reform efforts credible and criticised as 'irresponsible' proposals to zero out federal appropriations.[272] Says Doug Hellinger, executive director of Development Gap, 'Wolfensohn is still our last, best hope to bring about change'. The group that organised the 'Fifty Years is Enough' campaign now acts as a Bank consultant[273]

What's going on here? It is clear that environmental NGOs understand that only one aspect of the World Bank's power is the billions of dollars it lends.

---

[218] 'The Small Grants Program,' World Bank, 1997.
[219] 'Small Grants Program,' Final Statement of Grant Requests Approved – FY 1997, June 30, 1997.
[220] *Working with NGOs*, p. 50.
[271] Rich, *Mortgaging the Earth*, p. 315.
[272] 'World Bank Too Important To Be Left on Auto-Pilot, Says EDF; EDF Calls on Congress and Treasury Department To Strengthen Oversight on World Bank,' *EDF News Release*, March 27, 1995.
[273] Bruce Stokes, 'Wolfensohn's World,' *National Journal*, Vol. 29, No. 38, September 20, 1997 p. 1846.

The Bank is also an enforcer of international economic policy advice. By attaching conditions to its loans, it imposes its recommendations on borrower countries. Despite badly flawed structural adjustment policies that worsen poverty, NGOs do not want to give up the Bank's power to control the trade, industrial and fiscal policies of borrower countries[274]Seduced by World Bank grants, they seem determined to imagine the Bank as the instrument of their own purposes. Sadly, as they become influential insiders, the environmental NGOs lose interest in reforming a failed institution.

---

[274] Doug Bandow and Ian Vasquez, *Perpetuating Poverty*, (Washington: Cato Institute, 1995).

7. Prospects for the Future

Slowly but surely, the international environmental establishment is expanding. A global 'sustainable development' agenda is being implemented gradually at international conferences, treaty negotiations and follow-up meetings. International law is increasingly being shaped by what Green activists sometimes refer to as 'the process,' in which government officials and non-governmental organisations collaborate to produce mutually beneficial outcomes. International conferences produce timetables for the strengthening of government bureaucracies at the global level. The Clinton-Gore administration, the European Union, environmental grant-making foundations and the UN bureaucracy have each played vital roles in the process of forging international environmental law.

At the UN, millionaire Canadian diplomat and power broker Maurice Strong is once again important in environmental policymaking. For almost three decades, Strong has been a central figure in the international environmental movement. He launched the 1972 Stockholm conference and directed the 1992 Rio Earth Summit. Most recently, in January 1997, he was appointed special adviser to UN Secretary General Kofi Annan, charged with coordinating the world body's reform and restructuring efforts. He has also assumed a position on the board of Turner's UN Foundation.

Mounting NGO Frustration

All the pieces are seemingly in place for 'global governance' based on the environmentalist principles set forth at the 1992 Rio Earth Summit. Yet the legacy of the Earth Summit to date is a far cry from what its architects originally dreamed. The hoped-for burst of Western financial aid for sustainable development safeguards in poor countries did not materialise. Support for the UN is dwindling, both in financial and political terms.

In 1996, two irate NGOs issued harsh reports scolding the world's governments for not acting quickly enough. The Worldwatch Institute and the Costa Rica-based Earth Council, chaired by Maurice Strong, excoriated the US and other developed countries for failing to carry out *Agenda 21*. They took the US to task for failing to ratify the biodiversity treaty and for not providing enough foreign aid. The Earth Council lamented, 'It seems that nothing has changed for the better since 1992'.[221]

NGOs are seemingly annoyed at political leaders for breaching their commitments, but governments can only go so far without popular support. The unpleasant reality for many Green activists is that the global sustainable development plan is just not popular with the masses. Maurice Strong admitted as much when complained: 'Far too few countries, companies, institutions, communities and citizens have made the choices and changes needed to advance

---

[221] Maricel Sequeira, 'NGOs to Evaluate Earth Summit,' *Inter Press Service*, January 16, 1997.

the goals of sustainable development'.[222]

In March 1997, five hundred delegates and NGO representatives gathered in Rio to set the tone for a special June 1997 'Rio + 5' conference at the UN and to review the progress made on implementing the Agenda 21 agreement.[223] Strong explained that the second Earth Summit was 'designed to regenerate some of the momentum, which, to some degree has faltered'.[224] To do so, Rio + 5 organisers focused not only on government commitments, but on people's 'value systems'. An effective environmental agenda 'is unlikely to be the result of a single top-down plan,' commented Worldwatch Institute's Christopher Flavin.[225]

Despite the rhetoric, the urge for top-down planning remains. An elitist force, the international environmental establishment will not wait for a dramatic shift in public attitudes to take place. Most proponents of global environmentalism feel that their cause is too important to wait for public opinion. Without ever obtaining the consent of the people, the global Greens already have what they really want – power. Green activists, writes Philip Shabecoff, 'have forced their way into the previously closed rooms of international diplomacy'. The persistent pressure groups are 'placing their position papers on the table and speaking out, not just in the corridors but in the once sacrosanct plenary halls and in the small, out-of the-way chambers where deals a1re hammered out in secret meetings'.[226]

What should we anticipate

The Green 'sustainable development' agenda is firmly entrenched in international circles. UN officials, diplomats and NGO lobbyists will do their best to make sure it continues its relentless march forward. But, as the Rio + 5 meetings demonstrated, the global environment lobby's job is not nearly complete. Several follow-up actions can be expected from government agencies, the UN and environmental pressure groups.

The centre stage international environmental issue is global warming. The Kyoto Protocol agreed to in December 1997 seeks to bring the fluctuating global climate under control, using energy restrictions to cool the entire planet by several degrees. Secretary of State Albright announced 'a diplomatic full-court press to encourage meaningful developing country participation in the effort to combat global climate change'.[227] Such an effort is necessary because developing countries

---

[222] 'Little Progress Since Rio, Says Earth Council,' *Europe Environment*, January 14, 1997; David Briscoe, 'Worldwatch: World in Bad Shape,' *Associated Press*, January 12, 1997.

[223] Daniel J. Shephard, 'Ambitious Plans Mark Fifth Anniversary of Rio Parley,' *Earth Times*, December 22, 1996.

[224] Colin Macilwain, 'Rio Review to Rejuvenate Green Initiatives,' *Nature* Vol. 385, January 16, 1997, p. 188.

[225] Vicki Allen, 'Earth's Symptoms Worsen Since Rio Summit,' *Reuters European Community Report*, January 12, 1997.

[226] Philip Shabecoff, *A New Name for Peace: International Environmentalism, Sustainable Development and Democracy*, (Hanover, NH: University Press of New England, 1996) p. 76.

[227] Secretary of State Madeleine K. Albright, Remarks on Earth Day 1998 at the National Museum of Natural History, April 21, 1998.

have rejected economy-wrecking energy restrictions that would hamper their efforts to escape poverty. The US Senate will not ratify a global warming treaty that imposes economic hardship only on industrialised countries.

The international environmental establishment sought to forge some kind of compromise with the likes of India and China. At the 1998 Fourth Conference of the Parties in Buenos Aires, that compromise did not occur. Undeveloped nations refused even to consider shackling themselves to binding greenhouse gas emissions limitations. On the very first day of the meeting, the Group of 77 developing countries and China voted overwhelmingly to remove this item from the discussion agenda. No amount of cajoling could budge them from their steadfast positions, even promises of special consideration for foreign aid projects.

In other areas, the international environmental establishment will continue its push to undermine the sovereignty of nation states. The following international treaties have recently been concluded but remain to be ratified by certain signatory states (including the US):

> *The Biodiversity Convention.* Under the pretext of species protection, this treaty authorises increased government control of private land use. Plans already exist to extend its restrictions to biotechnology innovation, via a Biosafety Protocol.

> *The Basle Convention.* By defining various metals as 'hazardous,' this treaty controls trade in waste, scrap and recyclable materials. Greenpeace is using the treaty to organise a total embargo on trade with developing countries, excluding them from global scrap metal markets.

> *The Convention to Combat Desertification.* This treaty aims to prevent land degradation by giving $30 billion of foreign aid to African governments for 'anti-desertification' purposes. In the past, such aid has perpetuated land mismanagement by promoting centrally planned irrigation projects, subsidised farming and water usage and inept agro-forestry policies.[228]

> *The POPs Treaty.* As a result of pressure by environmental groups, governments of more than 150 countries are negotiating a binding global treaty to ban 'persistent organic pollutants,' defined as pesticides, industrial chemicals and their by-products. Certain pesticides crucial to the eradication of disease-carrying mosquitoes in the Third World, such as DDT, could be banned under the treaty.

Last but not least, the international environmental establishment has an

---

[228] See Julian Morris, *The Political Economy of Land Degradation: Pressure Groups, Foreign Aid and the Myth of Man-Made Deserts*, (London: Institute of Economic Affairs, 1995).

almost insatiable appetite for tax money. To finance burgeoning global bureaucracies, implement expanding treaty commitments and entice Third World regimes, the global Greens need significant amounts of cash. Government officials in developed countries, UN officials and their pressure group allies will lobby for increased appropriations to agencies such as the World Bank, the Global Environment Facility and national bilateral development agencies. They will also continue to advocate strengthening the United Nations system across the board by increasing funding of the world body.

Their success is not inevitable, however. Environmental pressure groups have bet heavily on mastering the bureaucratic processes and timetables of international conferences and agencies. Global greens have put their faith in the 'process.' They have achieved success even when their ideas have been discredited. What is needed now is the vigilance to detect their manoeuvrings and the skill to overcome them.